WE’RE HERE
AND WE’RE
QUEER
DYKE
DYKE
BAR

THE Dykonic HANDBOOK

THE ULTIMATE GUIDE TO
LIVING YOUR BEST QUEER LIFE

THE Dykonic HANDBOOK

AMY SPALDING

BLOOMSBURY PUBLISHING
LONDON • OXFORD • NEW YORK • NEW DELHI • SYDNEY

For my beautiful queer sisters, Sophie and Lucy

Proof that lightning can, in fact, strike thrice. I wish we had this book growing up.

Follow this QR code for the ultimate sapphic playlist

DYKONIC

dy·kon·ic

daɪ'kaː.nɪk / (dye-KON-ik)

adjective (informal/slang)

Portmanteau of the words 'dyke' and 'iconic', meaning exceptionally iconic within lesbian, sapphic or queer culture; embodying bold, confident or culturally resonant queer identity.

Intro-
duction

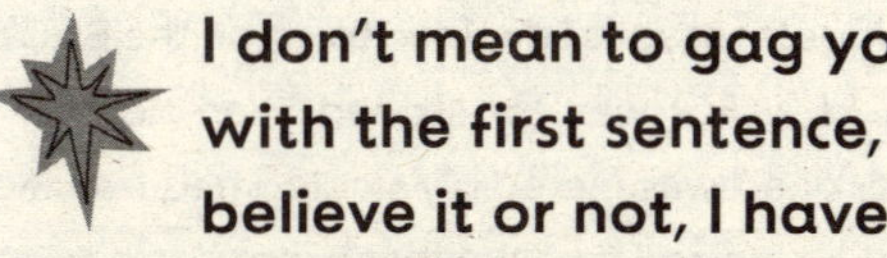

I don't mean to gag you with the first sentence, but believe it or not, I haven't always been screaming 'I'm a dyke' from the rooftops. In fact, if you'd have told sixteen-year-old me that I would one day write a book about all things lesbian, I would have said 'lower your damn voice' while waiting for the ground to swallow me up. Flashforward to today, I've lezzed out with girls on national television in nothing but boots and a bikini, and I spend my days posting about my lesbian antics on social media. Talk about doing a one-eighty.

One of the biggest reasons I decided to go on the BBC's *I Kissed a Girl* (*IKAG*) was for sixteen-year-old me. I mean, yes, for one, I was incredibly single. I had trawled the depths of Hinge and my own friendship circle to no avail, and was left with no other choice but to try more extreme methods. But on the other hand, I also knew how much a show with normalised representation like this would have meant to me and my sisters growing up.

I often say, if I were straight, I'd be unstoppable. Imagine every piece of media being directly relatable to you? Feeling sad? Lucky you – you have 32,729 girl-meets-boy films to choose from. Gay people have to choose between a low-budget French indie film made in 1978 or a minefield of harmful stereotypes. Growing up secretly gay in the 2000s and 2010s meant becoming an accidental archivist of your own erasure. While straight teenagers could passively absorb their existence through every single form of media to ever exist, we became digital archaeologists, gripping on to anything we could. We internalised a 'background noise' existence, this sense that our stories were perpetually 'almost', but never quite, the main event. So many of us lived on the internet instead, clutching at scraps like Ingrid Nilsen's coming-out video (IYKYK), paparazzi pics of Cara Delevingne and Ashley Benson carrying a sex swing, and Santana and Brittany's beautiful love story in *Glee*.

Back in 2016, while on a school trip to a trampoline park, someone flippantly mentioned how the current season of *Love Island* had a lesbian plotline brewing. For the rest of the trip, I was completely distracted. I drifted from trampoline to trampoline like a zombie, daydreaming about an evening filled with consuming brand-new lezzy content. Dream date. Each bounce was a step closer to getting home to the sweet embrace of my laptop screen. Finally, I got home and sprinted upstairs, my trampolining grippy socks aiding me in my journey across slippery hallway tiles and wooden stairs. I locked myself in my room and realised I had sixty episodes to catch up on. I couldn't just skip to today's episode, no, no, no. God forbid I miss any of the lore or build-up to the moment; that was all part of the satisfaction. I wasn't just a horny repressed lesbian teen who wanted to see two girls kiss. I had Tumblr for that. I needed the yearn, the context, the longing. Naturally, when the moment did finally happen, I rewound and watched it over and over again, so much so that I can picture the swing set that they kissed on in my mind's eye even today.

When the opportunity arose for me to be in what was essentially lesbian *Love Island*, and the UK's first sapphic dating show, this moment popped into my head. For so long, we thirsted over tiny drops of WLW plotline and settled for YouTube compilations of sapphic moments Frankensteined together. I knew that being a part of a show where we were the main event was an opportunity I couldn't pass up.

There was a moment towards the end of filming *IKAG* when the weight of what was about to unfold began to sink in. I was sitting on a sofa in the shade, getting a break from the Italian sun with one of the floor producers. Char and I had instantly clicked upon meeting, when I admired her Cate Blanchett tee. Both of us had queer siblings, and we both made being lesbian our entire personality. Like me, Char had absorbed every bit of lesbian lore and canon into her being, so much so that it was imprinted on her skin. Her arms and legs were painted with sapphic tattoos, my favourite depicting *that* scene from *Portrait of a Lady on Fire.* We would spend lunches seeing who could come up with the nichest lesbian reference from our minds' rolodexes, and unpacking each other's queer trauma in my chaperoned ciggy breaks. In this particular moment, I watched her eyes get wet as she talked about how important working on this show had been to her. Being a part of something so groundbreaking and the first of its kind will forever be her proudest achievement. I felt exactly the same.

Despite knowing this, nothing could have prepared me for the response when the show actually aired. I think it landed at exactly the right time. For years, lesbians have existed and demanded more conversations in the mainstream. An amalgamation of all the crumbs we'd settled for before bore down heavily on the floodgates. Soon, when they could no longer bear the weight of it all, a tidal wave of lezzy representation burst through.

A sapphic tsunami. The Lesbian Renaissance. All of a sudden, the word 'lesbian' was on everyone's lips. Dykes were crowned the It Girls we always knew we were, and the mainstream started taking note.

With sapphic powerhouses dominating the music scene, including Chappell Roan, Doechii, Reneé Rapp, Cat Burns and Kehlani, to name but a few, it seems every week a new celebrity comes out as queer in some capacity. Billie Eilish released a sexy anthem about eating a girl out. I mean, times don't get much better than this. We've even had an abundance of sapphic films and TV shows light up our screens that don't just centre around the trauma of coming out. Hurrah!

The astounding reaction to this waterfall of representation being lapped up by the masses shows to what extent we were dying of thirst. A testament to the statement 'you can't be what you can't see'. Even now, I receive DMs daily from people telling me how much *IKAG* meant to them, and how seeing normalised representation and girls being their queer selves unashamedly meant people felt seen and, for some, even comfortable enough to come out. With each message, a part of my inner child, crushed by the closet walls, heals a little more.

I've been fortunate enough to take on the role of an older sapphic sister of sorts to a few people through this platform I've been given. People come to me for queer advice, to vent or to join in the queer cultural discourse, and it makes my heart beam. I've already played this part at home with my sisters, and I know there's plenty more room under this wing!

This isn't a role I take lightly, and it's ultimately what led me to write this book. I wanted to put together the Big Sister Guide to sapphic life that I wish I had growing up. A source of sapphic celebration, because there is so much to celebrate. I will hold your hand through the trials and tribulations of coming out, and set you up to successfully traverse TikTok comments (beware: hey mamas lesbians ahead). We will embark on a journey through the history of queer dress and explore how to build your very own lesbian capsule wardrobe. With the help of some hilarious, anonymous, sexy-time stories, we will settle any nerves you may have before doing the deed, and then discover a plethora of new ways to find community, help you navigate the infamous lesbian web, and a whole lot more. This is a pocket-sized, one-stop shop that covers everything you need to know to help you become your best queer self.

Whether you're just embarking on your sapphic journey, are a fully fledged member of the queer community, or fit somewhere in between, this is the ultimate guide to navigating queerness in the modern age, and your very own handbook to being absolutely DYKONIC.

DYKE
BAR →

CHAPTER 1

Coming

FOR SOME QUEER PEOPLE, COMING OUT IS THIS ALL-CONSUMING, CATACLYSMIC EVENT THAT CHANGES EVERYTHING; OTHERS DON'T FIND THAT COMING OUT HAS THE SAME WEIGHT FOR THEM, AND SIMPLY FEEL THAT THEY CAN BYPASS THE FUSS.

The concept of 'coming out of the closet' is often seen as one of the most pivotal moments for a person in their queer journey. We've consumed a million films, shows and books in which coming out is the central premise: the singular, most important, all-consuming thing in a baby queer's life. But why is it that we even have to come out in the first place?

Unfortunately, at the time of writing, we live in a society that assumes heterosexuality is the default orientation. You are straight until proven gay. There's a theory named compulsive heterosexuality, or comphet for short, that breaks this down perfectly. Coined by feminist dykon Adrienne Rich, compulsive heterosexuality is the notion that heterosexuality is the norm in a society governed by patriarchy. That even if you do not necessarily feel attracted to the opposite gender, you work from the assumption that you are attracted to them, until proven otherwise. Comphet (while being a beautiful name for a baby girl) affirms the idea that in a society where it is the default to be heterosexual and cis, everything else is wrong, thereby villainising queer people and perpetuating homophobia. In a comphomo society (a girl can dream), the standard would be that straight people would have to come out. Imagine... now that's a little bit of me!

Whereas for some queer people, coming out is this all-consuming, cataclysmic event that changes everything, others don't find that coming out has the same weight for them, and simply feel that they can bypass the fuss. As is the case with all elements of a queer person's journey, this is completely individual and largely depends on the person's environment and situation.

My Own Coming Out

At school, I was your typical straight teenage girl. I had a constant string of boyfriends, all while being completely and totally obsessed with women and lesbian culture as a whole. Totally normal behaviour for a straight girl, right? Well, in my household, it was. Unbeknownst to us at the time, my sisters and I were fighting for elbow room in the closet. All three of us were 'straight', and our collective obsession with lesbian plotlines and lesbian YouTubers was a very normal and straight thing to do because we were very normal and straight.

We gushed over Emily from *Pretty Little Liars* at the dinner table and held each other when Shannon and Cammie broke up. The music video for 'Girls Like Girls' by Hayley Kiyoko played on a YouTube loop on the family computer, because the melody is great and the creative direction is, like, really cool or whatever. It had absolutely nothing to do with the fact that all three of us were repressed in our sexuality and related wholly to the plot of yearning for women in a straight world.

At seventeen, the cracks started to show. I was incredibly privileged to have such a great education, but this existed in a very conservative environment. There wasn't a single out 'n' proud person at school, and the one boy who was obviously gay was bullied and ridiculed for being effeminate. My surroundings were void of any positive queer representation, and I absorbed that completely, forcing me further into the closet. I spent parties crying my eyes out after one too many blue WKDs because I felt so alien in my desires. I would look at the girls around me, knowing that I wanted to kiss them and that they didn't feel the same way back. I had boyfriends that I was indifferent about, but my day would be ruined if I didn't get to cross paths with my girl crush at school. One time, at a party, I broke down in my best friend's arms, and when she asked what was wrong, I whispered 'I think I'm bisexual' into her chest. We didn't speak about it again until I came out fully at twenty-one.

My first year university clubbing experience consisted of me necking VKs to make out with boys and hopefully land myself on the 'Lacrossip Girl' Facebook page. The perfect way to secure a slice of that comphet validation pie I desperately craved. I would then scuttle back to my accommodation alone, kebab in hand, and rewatch the *The 100* solely for the lesbian plotline between Clarke and Lexa. The closet was glass, but I chose to bury my head in the sand, which, for a lot of my first year of university, was the hairy chest of the boy next door. I believed that because I could kiss boys there was no way that I was gay, despite following at least three 'CLEXA' fan pages on Instagram. With the post-coming out clarity I now possess, I see with 20/20 vision a million clues to my queerness, and I wonder how I could have been so blind to it back then. Baby girl, no straight person shaves their vulva for the Hayley Kiyoko concert.

Despite knowing all of this deep down, I refused to actually ask myself if I was a lesbian. Coming out wasn't an option, even to myself. Besides, I thought maybe if I was a teeny tiny bit bi, I would end up with a man anyway, so there was no point putting myself and my family through the whiplash of coming out. I had made peace with a future of overconsuming lesbian culture in the shadows and cosplaying as straight to the world. But then I fell in love and everything changed.

My first girlfriend essentially dragged me kicking and screaming out of the closet, and if it weren't for her, maybe I never would have left it. She saw right through the transparent closet walls, clocking onto the blindingly obvious obsession I had with all things lezzy. I mean, it doesn't take a rocket scientist. The love that we shared gave me the courage to come out, as I wanted to share that love and part of myself with the people I loved most in this world. Although the thought scared me shitless, the thought of losing her scared me more, so I jumped.

I wish I could say it went swimmingly, but it didn't. I came out to Mum at the dinner table, exclaiming that I had something to tell her, to which she responded jokingly with, 'You're not gay, are you?' I broke down crying, and my sister (who feared Mum's reaction to her own coming out in the future) cried as well, begging my mum to hug me, which she refused to do. Mum grew up in a very traditional household with a super

Irish-Catholic father. This, combined with my femme presentation and endless string of boyfriends at school, meant she was understandably knocked for six by this new revelation. Over the next couple of years, my sisters followed suit, and the closet became akin to a comical clown car. It hasn't been a super easy journey, but with time, Mum has adjusted to this new reality and has let go of the futures she had predicted for us. I can see that she has come an incredibly long way since that conversation at the dinner table, and I am so proud of her ability to grow and learn. Today, she welcomes our partners with open arms and gushes to her friends about how proud she is of us.

I am now out to people I never even considered it an option to come out to. I always shied away from the idea of telling Grandma, because I didn't want to send her into an early grave. But my hand was forced when *I Kissed a Girl* (IKAG) was going to air. Had I not told her, she may have accidentally flipped the channel to BBC Three and seen me necking on with a girl while in the Masseria. Being on IKAG meant that I inadvertently came out to everyone from my past as well, including people I wasn't in touch with at the time. After the show aired, so many people from my past came out of the woodwork to tell me they were so proud of me and inspired by my journey. Trauma = healed.

THE RIGHT WAY FOR YOU

For me, coming out was always going to be this huge song and dance, but this isn't the case for everyone. My friend Hannah, a butch lesbian rugby player, never felt the need to formally come out: 'I've always been very openly queer. I was told before I even knew myself, so no one was surprised when I came out. I'm pretty sure my mum's friends actually had a sweepstake on whether I was gonna be gay or not, and I'm pretty sure 99 per cent of them picked that I was gonna be gay.'

There is no one-size-fits-all method when it comes to coming out. But the cool thing is that you'll have to do it again and again and again, so you can really experiment with a lot of different methodologies and see what works for you. I don't mean to scare you, but this is just the reality of a queer life lived in a comphet society. You are presumed straight until proven otherwise, remember!

Of course, who you choose to come out to is completely up to you. For a certain, select group of people in your life, this might be hard. Maybe they are the first people you have told, maybe they are the people whose opinion you care about the most, maybe they're strict or judgemental or have views that conflict with yours. These coming-outs will have to be more thought out, and may be more serious. Sometimes the coming out will be easy. You'll be walking down the street with your girlfriend holding hands and run into a colleague.

You'll say offhandedly, '*Kim Possible* was my sexual awakening,' to a high school friend. You'll be standing in a dyke bar, and that hot girl from your Pilates class will walk in.

There are no rules to getting out of the closet, but there are definitely some things you should consider beforehand:

* **You don't have to come out to everyone at once.**
* **Come up with a plan of what you're going to say, how and who to. Choose someone you really trust. If they are someone who is more likely to take it well, then that's a good place to start. It makes it easier to build on positive experiences.**
* **Your safety is paramount. Is this a safe person to come out to?**

Don't forget, even if you're the only person who knows about your gender identity or sexuality, it is still 100 per cent real and valid. For some people, coming out isn't an option. Coming out could put their finances, housing situation or their physical safety at risk. If this is the case for you, your safety should be your top priority. If coming out isn't an option, you are not less than for choosing to protect yourself. This is absolutely something that can wait.

A MILLION AND ONE WAYS

I asked my lovely Instagram followers for their own coming-out stories, and boy, did they deliver. Here are some of my favourites.

You can make coming out as big or as little of a deal as you want. If you're an attention whore (hey!), feel free to fly Liza Minnelli out for a one-woman musical told from the perspective of your sapphic interior life for all your nearest and dearest. Molly, one of my Instagram followers, chose a lower key, more budget-friendly option. One summer's evening, sitting in the backyard with her mum, she finally decided it was time. When she told her she was gay, her mum paused and said, 'Do you know what, I have always thought Sue Perkins was a fox. More wine?'

For another follower, Naomi, her coming out was also on the less dramatic end of the scale. She texted her parents letting them know that she is pansexual. Her mum reacted with a meme of a pan, and her dad said: 'Oh yeah, we knew.'

For some, a catalyst helps. Charlotte first understood that she was gay aged thirteen, but it wasn't until she was diagnosed with cancer at twenty-six that she decided to come out. 'Cancer took away the comfort of someday. There was no longer an indefinite future where I could be braver later, or more honest when the timing felt right. Continuing to hide felt more frightening than telling the truth.' Then, while undergoing chemotherapy, she met her future wife. They dated while Charlotte was in treatment, and in the quiet spaces in between appointments. 'Loving her didn't change my diagnosis, but it changed everything else. It taught me that even in uncertainty, there could be joy. That even in illness, there could be love. And that honesty, however late it arrives, is never wasted.'

For Briagha, her partner's coming out enabled her own. She had always known deep down she was attracted to women but had only dated men, in classic comphet style. She got into a relationship with a man, who then, four years later, told Briagha she was trans. 'It was confusing at first, but very quickly I grew to understand I was actually very attracted to her femininity.' Another four years later, and they're happily married, living in sapphic bliss. 'It was a blessing because it gave me, a serial monogamist, the opportunity to explore the queer part of myself, which I never would've been able to do if it wasn't for her bravery.'

For others, each coming out led to a new understanding of themselves, and in some cases, another coming out again. Ez is no stranger to coming out. They came out initially as bisexual to their bestie at the age of twelve. After dating a series of girls in their teens, they came out as a lesbian at the age of seventeen. When they arrived at uni, they began to expand their queer knowledge, understanding more about the trans community and coming out as non-binary. Now, turning twenty-five, they don't know what they are. Trans masc? Non-binary? Bisexual? All feel possible. 'I'm happy, and I'm queer, and that's all that matters.'

Ez's story reminded me a bit of my friend Elios, who has come out multiple times as his identity and understanding of himself shifted and evolved over the years. He first came out as bi at fourteen, then as a lesbian, as gender fluid when he was sixteen, and finally as a trans man at seventeen. Since then, it's mostly stayed the same. He's still a trans man, and still bisexual. 'When it comes to coming out, finally finding the language to describe how you feel, and taking on that label, is so empowering. Being able to say it with your full chest and owning it. I remember so well as a trans person growing up in a small town by the south coast that I felt super isolated. I'm deaf as well, so I truly felt one of a kind – the only person I knew who was like me. Someone who prayed at age ten every night to wake up as a boy, and who tried his absolute best to become more feminine, to fit in with the other girls. It was scary and lonely, and I was so aware my parents wouldn't understand it (thankfully they do now – there's hope!). Finding the word 'trans' many years later was so important because all of those years of dysphoria, especially hitting hard when I went through puberty, finally made sense.'

Elios makes another good point, which is that sometimes people come out and realise the word they used wasn't the right word for them: 'It's important to never feel like once you've come out as something, that it's set in stone, or a commitment. I find it adds a pressure that shouldn't be pushed on anyone. We all need time to settle into our skin, and that can take as long as it needs. Experimenting with your pronouns, talking to a counsellor or peers, looking for YouTube videos or BOOKS LIKE THIS ONE, are a great way of figuring out and breathing easy through the coming out process.'

Hey, thanks for the shout out! In all seriousness, he has a point. As we discover more about ourselves and uncover more queer language, it's very possible that how we identify ourselves will change. For some people, this means they prefer to go label-less entirely.

When Scarlett was thirteen, she came out for the first time as bisexual. She spent a lot of time feeling like she wasn't 'gay enough', as someone who was feminine-presenting and not entirely sure who she was attracted to. She found her self-esteem and confidence fading, so she tried on the lesbian label, but found it constricted her world, instead of expanding it. Now aged twenty, she prefers to leave her sexuality undefined: 'I love my girlfriend, and that's all that matters to me.' Same, Scarlett, same.

Coming out, however you choose to do it, can be challenging. But I can promise you this: it will also be powerful, it will be special, it will help you unlock your full potential, and it will help you find community. We're here, waiting for you.

CHAPTER 2

Key Queer Term-inology

SO YOU TOOK A SIXTY-FOUR-QUESTION BUZZFEED QUIZ AND IT TURNS OUT YOU'RE A 100-FOOTER, FUTCH LESBIAN WITH BLACK CAT TENDENCIES AND AN URGE TO MERGE, BUT WHAT ON EARTH DOES ANY OF THAT MEAN?!

Navigating sapphic lingo is no easy feat; like the English language, it is forever changing and adapting to the times. A lot of current queer culture is rooted in the social and cultural zeitgeist, with a heavy emphasis on what's happening in online spaces, so naturally, this is reflected in how we speak, as we adopt these new terms and references to better communicate within our community. This language evolution seems to be happening at an exponential rate as our attention spans get shorter and the queers get more creative.

You may be wondering why there is such a big old gay dictionary. Well, historically, we queers had to develop our own lavender language as a survival mechanism, helping us fly under the radar in public, fostering community and resisting against a homophobic society. We have our Black and trans siblings to thank for the majority of queer vernacular used today, and it is necessary to recognise their genius and the impact they've had upon the community's ability to express ourselves and our culture when using it.

In an attempt to widen my research pool for this chapter, I put a call out on my Instagram story for people to send in their favourite lesbian slang terms; call that journalism. This proved both bountiful and wildly confusing. Picture me hunched over in bed at 3 a.m., bathed in the blue glow from my laptop screen, frantically googling 'bean queen' to no avail. One submission consisted of only the word 'lasagna'...

I was also inundated with sapphic euphemisms for sex, all of which were too good not to share. So, next time you're telling a story and are looking for a creative way to let your mates know that you were doing the deed with that dyke you met on Hinge, maybe try one of the following phrases to spice up your vernacular:

* Bumpin' purses
* Lip synching
* Coochie bumpin'
* Clam bumpin'
* DJ to the VJ
* Clam bashin'
* Bumpin' brillos
* Muffin bumpin'
* Bumpin' bush
* Pinging the prawn (wtf?)
* Lip locking
* Smashing pasties
* Beaver bumpin'
* Sesbian lex
* Clam jousting
* Clit clankin' (a personal fave)

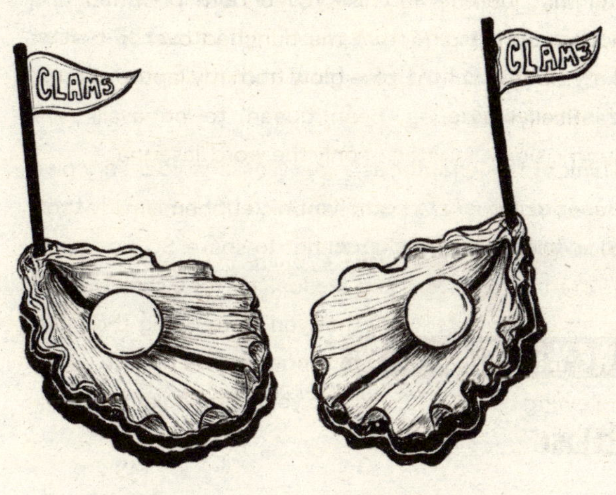

There seems to be lots of bashin' and bumpin'... I guess people are cruisin' for a bruisin'.'

The lesbian lexicon is wide-ranging. It can be as simple as knowing the difference between 'femme' and 'masc', but you may have come across other words that aren't as obvious at first glance. Not every term does precisely what it says on the tin; for example, spending £950 on a pair of Diesel boots does not make you a 'diesel dyke', something I learned the hard way. Navigating this can be very daunting for anyone, let alone a baby queer who hasn't a clue what a baby queer is. Unfortunately, there is no lezza language option on Duolingo (yet!). So if you're still trying to work out what the fuck a 'hey mamas lesbian' is and how you can avoid one, fear not: you've come to the right place! Your big sapphic sister Amy is here to hold your hand and guide you through this lexical maze.

Think of this chapter as a gay glossary: your very own queer dictionary to equip you with the necessary tools to speak the native tongue.

WE WILL START EASY:

Masc

A queer person who presents more traditionally masculine.

Femme

A queer person who is more (you guessed it) feminine presenting. There is some debate about spelling, and the difference between 'femme' and 'fem'. In this book, I use femme to mean a feminine-presenting lesbian or queer person.

NOW HERE'S WHERE THINGS GET A LITTLE MORE COMPLICATED:

Butch

Butch is an identity used by some masculine-presenting queer people. Think of 'masc' as more of an umbrella term for masculine gender expression, whereas 'butch' is more of a cultural identity with a deep-rooted history. All butches are masc, but not all mascs are butches. Some notable examples of butches in popular culture include, Big Boo from *Orange is the New Black*; Carrie in the *L-Word* reboot (played by Rosie O'Donnell, a dykonic butch in her own right); and Anne Lister in *Gentleman Jack* (based on a real person, see page 76).

If you want real people, there's k.d. lang, Jenny Shimizu, Grace Petrie...

Masc 4 masc

Or 'butch 4 butch'. A queer who presents as more masculine and is looking for a masculine partner.

Femme 4 femme

Or, as I put it, 'fam for fam', with extra vocal fry. This term will follow me until I die, thanks to my time on *I Kissed a Girl*, where the edit made it seem like these were the only words that left my posh little mouth while living in the Masseria. This describes an individual who is more femme-presenting and is also looking for a more femme-presenting partner.

Futch

A portmanteau of the two words 'femme' and 'butch'. Also known as **chapstick lesbians**, they're likely to be in the middle of the spectrum, presenting a mix of both traditionally feminine and masculine expressions. Unlikely to step out of the house with their faces beat to the gawds but wouldn't be afraid of a light make-up look and a bit of chapstick, hence their namesake. Think Kristen Stewart.

Soft masc

Or soft butch, someone who leans more masculine with a feminine gentleness incorporated into their mannerisms or aesthetic.

Stud

A term exclusively used by the Black community that refers to a masculine-presenting lesbian. Similar to butch, this term has a deep-rooted social and cultural history. Stud doesn't just mean a butch who is Black, but is in its own right a whole separate identity.

Stem

Another portmanteau combining 'stud' and 'femme'. Like a futch, stem describes a blend of these terms and is exclusively used by the Black community.

Top, bottom & vers (switch)

In the sapphic community, these terms have a much broader, looser meaning than in the gay male community from which we have adopted them. They relate to one's role during intimacy.

A **top** is someone who generally likes to take the lead in the bedroom and prefers to give sexually. *Alexa, play Chappell Roan's 'The Giver'.* However, they aren't averse to receiving.

A **bottom** is someone who likes to take the back seat and receive pleasure from the top; however, they aren't opposed to putting in a shift now and then.

A **vers** (short for versatile) or **switch** will play for both sides depending on their partner and mood.

HERE'S SOME MORE VOCABULARY YOU MIGHT COME ACROSS:

100-footer

Someone you can tell is queer from a hundred feet away, although I'd argue this is getting harder as the straights have discovered jorts and carabiners.

Baby queer

(A.k.a. baby gay or baby dyke.) A newly out queer person who has just started their journey into exploring their sexuality. Baby queers can sometimes unfairly be perceived negatively by seasoned lesbians who have no interest in being an experiment; however, we all have to start our journey somewhere.

Black cat

The antithesis of the golden retriever trope (see page 45). Often goes in tandem with femme-ness, although, as with the golden retriever, it's more a personality trait than a look. Black cats are independent individuals with an edge. Mysterious and sexy, this trope can read as standoffish and cold, but really, they're just self-sufficient baddies.

Celesbian

This one's pretty obvious: a celebrity or well-known figure who is a lesbian. Interchangeable with the term 'dykon' (or 'bicon', for all the bisexual icons out there).

Clam jamming

A sapphic twist on the hetero term 'cock blocking'. When one's attempt at pursuing a potential suitor is thwarted by a fellow sapphic. Another great synonym for this is 'cliterference'.

Comphet

New drinking game unlocked: drink every time the queers make a new portmanteau. This one combines 'compulsory' and 'heterosexuality', referring to the fact that everything in society is assumed cis and straight until proven otherwise (see page 20).

Diesel dyke

Very butch and typically strong, this hunk of a dyke is the antithesis of the male gaze and is oh-so-hot for it. Seen as very tough or rugged, their name is said to be derived from diesel engines, emphasising power and strength. Not quite the picture of me in the aforementioned knee-high Diesel stiletto boots.

Dom femme

Utilising an abbreviation of the word 'dominant', this term is big on TikTok and describes a femme who 'wears the trousers' in a relationship (probably while rocking a skirt). They're in charge, whether that's in the bedroom or just in day-to-day life. As a femme-for-femme who hates to think for herself, I myself am particularly inclined to a dom femme.

Dopplebanger

You know those two dykes that are dating, but they look like they once shared the same womb? That's a dopplebanger. It's giving siblings or dating, level: impossible. A fun synonym that I've seen crop up a few times is 'dykealike'.

Enby

Phonetic pronunciation for the acronym NB, which stands for non-binary and refers to a person whose gender falls outside the male-female binary. These folk typically use they/them pronouns (see page 62).

Gold star

A lesbian who has never been with a man before. An outdated term that has biphobic and transphobic connotations.

Golden retriever

Similar to their namesake, these individuals are bubbly, full of positive energy, and are just happy to be involved. Although sometimes a little needy, their playful and loveable charm prevails. Although usually falling on the masc end of the spectrum, I'd argue that 'golden retriever' is more of a vibe one gives and could apply to anyone.

Grandmother of pearl

An older lesbian. This one is unverified, with the only source being an Instagram DM I received; however, I love it so much I'd like to see it catch on and therefore have given it permanent residence in this not-so-official gay glossary.

Granola lesbian

Loves sunrise yoga, açai bowls and hikes. You'll find this Earth-loving queer thrifting an outfit or perusing their local farm shop in a pair of second-hand Birkenstocks. They probably go indoor climbing on the weekends and most definitely own a Hydro Flask. The Greta Thunberg of dykes.

Hey mamas

Considered the 'fuck boy' of the lesbian community, a 'hey mamas' lesbian is more of a personality type than a look. However, if you had to describe their aesthetic, they would generally be sporting any or all of the following: a backwards cap, a sports bra, a high bun, and an undercut. You'll often find a 'hey mamas' thirst trapping on TikTok. Picture a cringy lip bite, hands rubbing together, maybe a coy smile and a slight nod to the camera as they let out a 'hey mama' as their attempt at courtship.

Lesbian bed death (LBD)

This is the myth that lesbian couples are more likely to reach a point in their relationship where shared sexual intimacy slows down or even stops. This term is rooted in misogyny and homophobia, as 'bed death' can happen in any relationship, regardless of sexual orientation.

Lipstick lesbian

Also known as a high femme, this refers to a person whose self-expression sits right at the end of the feminine side of the spectrum. Think long cunty acrylics, face beat, high heels on their tippies and great gowns! Beautiful gowns! Can often be found battling the 'well, you don't look like a lesbian' pricks at their local.

Lululesbian

I hadn't heard this one before either, don't worry. Upon further research (doomscrolling on social media), this appears to be a lesbian who only wears Lululemon or Lululemon-style workout gear. Typically femme presenting, you'll catch them not in a gym, but instead lip-synching to a Reneé Rapp song on TikTok in cycling shorts and that viral Lululemon zip-up everyone was going crazy for in 2021. There's a fifty-fifty chance they're carrying either a Hydro Flask or an iced drink from Starbucks. Looking back, I was definitely a Lululesbian in 2017, but was too far in the closet to realise.

Pillow princess

Also known as a stone bottom or stone femme (for those feminine-presenting), this is the sexual complement to the stone top. This is someone who only likes to receive during intimacy and does not perform sexual acts on their partner. Often unfairly deemed lazy or selfish, pillow princesses are misunderstood; being a bottom requires both stamina and vulnerability. This is a sexual preference, and like all boundaries within sex, should be respected, not shamed.

Pocket masc

Proof that good things come in small packages. A smaller (generally 5 ft. 2 or under) masc-presenting queer who you want to put in your pocket to take wherever you go. Short kings rise up.

Power bottom

This is someone who receives during sexual relations but is definitely not submissive. A power bottom is what a coxswain is to a crew of rowers. They do none of the heavy lifting themselves, but take control by co-ordinating the 'rower's' power and rhythm, 'providing commands for steering, safety and race strategy'. Think of them as an enthusiastic cheerleader who's a little bossy; I should know.

Sapphic

A woman or non-binary individual attracted to other women or non-binary people. Derived from OG dykon Sappho, who lived on the Greek island of Lesbos in the sixth century BCE. It's thanks to her and her WLW poetry that the island became synonymous with female homosexuality – the original Scissor City, if you will.

Scissor City

Now here is a niche one, which, unless you're chronically online (like me), will probably make zero sense. This TikTok term is often used as follows: 'I went to Scissor City and everyone said they knew you'. Think of Scissor City as a metaphorical haven, where one gains automatic citizenship simply by being a part of the sapphic community. One-way ticket, please!

Stone top

Someone who exclusively likes to give during intimacy and derives their pleasure from satisfying their partner, with little to no interest in receiving sexual acts. This term does not refer to the gender expression of a person; however, butches with these sexual preferences may be referred to as a 'stone butch' or a 'touch me not'. A 'stone femme', however, is a stone bottom (see Pillow Princess on page 48), not a feminine-presenting stone top – confusing, I know...

Tribbing

Time to get sexy. This is a term I hadn't even realised I'd been putting into action until I looked up the definition. Tribbing is the sexual act of rubbing one's genitals on another's body, either on their genitals or literally anywhere else that you both find hot. This could be their leg, arms, tummy or even their face – wherever feels good, as long as you are both comfortable and consenting. Scissoring is a form of tribbing, but not all kinds of tribbing are scissoring. The best part about tribadism is its body and gender inclusivity, allowing everyone to get in on the fun.

U-Haul

That couple whose first date turned into a five-day sleepover, and by the end of it, they were scrolling through Rightmove for a flat together and debating whether to call the cat they just adopted Shane or Bette. That's U-Hauling. This term is derived from the name of the American moving company, and plays off the stereotype that sapphics move quickly in a relationship and would likely have the U-Haul packed and ready to move in with each other after the second date.

The urge to merge

A lesbian trope that suggests the longer a couple is together, the more similar they become to each other. As lesbian relationships stereotypically move quicker than hetero ones, this happens at an exponential rate. From shared wardrobes to shared mannerisms, two become one. The other day, I walked in on my lesbian roommate (who is also my ex, duh) sitting on her girlfriend's lap while she was having a wee. A step too far? I do think.

WLW

An acronym for 'women loving women', meaning sapphic in any capacity. This term is often used phonetically as 'wuhluhwuh' and is popular on TikTok as a hashtag to let people know that one is for the girls. Someone may post a thirst trap with the caption '#wlw', and another will comment, 'There's my favourite hashtag!'.

And there you have it: Amy's Big Gay Glossary all in one place, although I do not doubt that since the time of writing, a million more terms have popped up online with even more niche references. However, I hope any baby gays who were feeling a little overwhelmed in queer spaces feel better equipped to hold their own. Or, at the very least, have an easier time understanding comments on WLW TikTok. Happy tribbing!

CHAPTER 3

Labels

OK, SO YOU KNOW YOU LIKE GIRLS. SO, YOU'RE A LESBIAN? WELL, DEFINITELY AT LEAST BI... OR, ACTUALLY, DOES PAN MAKE MORE SENSE?! SHALL WE JUST RUN WITH QUEER? OR IS THAT NOT SITTING AS SPECIFICALLY AS YOU WANT IT TO?

Labels can be restrictive for those who don't feel like they fit neatly into perfect definitions, but figuring out you're somewhere on the spectrum is the first step. And for some people, that's enough.

It helps to imagine queer labels as umbrellas to sit under, rather than boxes with no elbow room or space for growth. We've only just come out of the closet, let's not confine ourselves again so soon!

Personally, exploring labels helped me further understand my own sexual attraction and gender identity. For those who, like me, beg for a little more specificity and prefer to put a name to a face, or in this case, a label to a sexuality and/or gender identity, then understanding the LGBTQIA+ alphabet soup is crucial. So, pick up a spoon and let's get stuck in!

BUT FIRST, A LITTLE HISTORY LESSON...

We haven't always had this handy little acronym, which brings together all whose gender and sexuality sit outside the hetero-cis norm. Some (me) would say the story of Genesis in the Bible parallels the genesis of the acronym in this here Dyke Bible.

At first, there was only G, and all who did not conform to the het-cis norm were labelled Gay.

Then we said 'let there be light!', and Lesbians were added.

Bisexual was bestowed upon the acronym for those who were unfairly excluded because they liked it all.

Then T was added and debated over for not being a sexuality, but rather involving gender identity. Trans activists, specifically trans women of colour such as Sylvia Rivera and Marsha P. Johnson, have long been at the forefront of the fight for our community's rights and inclusion. Thus, T remains firmly in its place, as it should. Let me be very clear: there is no LGB without the T!

But wait, if my maths is correct, it should be GLBT, right? Well, in the 1980s, the L got bumped to the front to honour the vital role lesbians played in supporting the community during the AIDS crisis. Society at large had turned its back on those suffering due to the incorrect assumption that this disease affected only gay men and other marginalised folk. Prejudices saw governments ignoring the issue, doctors and nurses refusing to treat patients, and even families abandoning those who were sick. This left an uncountable number of people vulnerable, and as such, dykes stepped up in their masses. They cared for and nursed the ill, took to the streets to protest for government action, organised blood drives and often gave blood during critical shortages as gay men were banned from donating. And that's on community!

Q was added as the fifth letter, for 'Queer' or 'Questioning', to include those who want to explore their gender and sexuality outside of a rigidly defined label. Following this, we welcomed I for Intersex and A for Asexual or Aromantic to the family and, of course, the +, which acts as a permanent invitation to anyone else who wants to join the kiki.

And on the seventh and final day, we rested. Except we didn't, as the fight for equal rights and inclusion is not yet over.

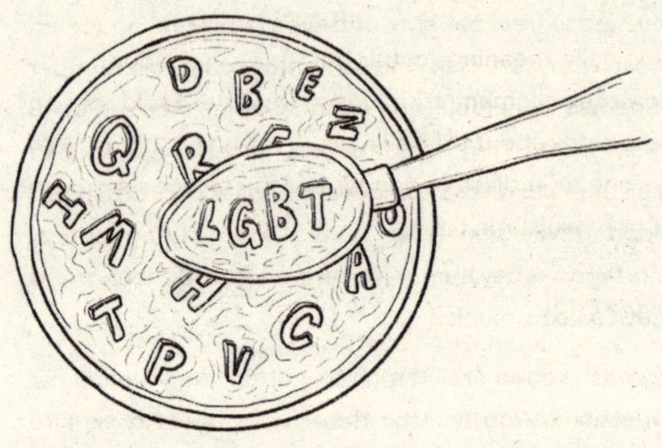

THE ABCS OF THAT DAMN ALPHABET SOUP

Lesbian

If you've picked up this book, I'll assume you're well aware that lesbian = female homosexuality. Well, yes! Traditionally this was the case, and if you look up lesbian in the Oxford English Dictionary, you'll get the same answer, but rejecting norms and 'tradition' is something we queer folk do best. The intersection of gender, sexuality and identity is wonderfully complicated and beautifully messy. Maybe you initially identified as a lesbian woman, but then the 'woman' part didn't feel right. This doesn't mean you have to let go of the lesbian part as well; that identity is still yours, should it still resonate with you. If the Doc Martens still fits...

Gay

Originally meaning joyful, this term was adopted by homosexual men as a code word to avoid raising suspicions about their sexuality. Nowadays, it's used by anyone regardless of gender to refer to one's sexuality as homosexual in nature.

Bisexual

Activist, speaker and all round bicon (bisexual icon to the uninitiated), Robyn Ochs describes bisexuality as 'the potential to be attracted romantically and/or sexually to people of more than one sex and/or gender, not necessarily at the same time, not necessarily in the same way, and not necessarily to the same degree.' Period!

Robyn's definition is MUY IMPORTANTE as it updates the outdated falsity that bisexuality means you can only be attracted to two genders. Back in the olden days, Western society didn't have a great understanding of the spectrum of gender and therefore used the prefix that means 'two'. Now, we understand bisexuality to mean attraction to more than one gender. Hurrah!

Rumoured bisexual and ~~daddy~~ father of the sexual revolution Albert Kinsey created a scale to show the spectrum of bisexuality. Named, innovatively, the Kinsey Scale, it runs from 0 (exclusively heterosexual) to 7 (100 per cent homo), and everything in between labels you a bisexual baddie.

Transgender

While we are in the game of understanding acronyms, here are two more to sink your teeth into: AFAB and AMAB, meaning Assigned Female At Birth and Assigned Male At Birth, respectively.

If you're trans, your gender identity doesn't align with what sex you were assigned at birth. Where being a lesbian, gay or bi is a sexuality and refers to who you are attracted to, your gender identity is who you *are.*

Everyone has a gender identity, regardless of whether you are trans or not, but most people don't think too deeply about it because they already identify with what they were assigned at birth. When I was born, the doctor looked at my parts, said, 'Yup, she's a girl,' and sent me on my merry way. As I grew, so did my sense of self, and because my developing gender identity never strayed from what I was assigned, I now live my life as a woman, answering to she/her pronouns. A trans man, however, may be AFAB, but upon developing his sense of self, realises he doesn't align with this misdiagnosis and may thenceforth live as he truly is – as a man.

Like sexuality, gender identity can be thought of as a spectrum. All cis and some transgender people sit at one end of the spectrum as women and men, but other trans people don't fit neatly into this female–male binary. These baddies have adopted the apt term 'non-binary', and their gender identity is expressed as either both male and female, or neither. Some non-binary people may identify as trans femme or trans masc, meaning their gender expression leans more towards one end of the binary, while still not identifying as being either female or male. For example, a trans masc person doesn't identify as a female or male but does feel their gender identity is more masculine. They might opt for he/they or they/them pronouns. A trans femme person doesn't identify as a female and is non-binary, but feels their gender identity is more feminine and might opt for she/they pronouns.

Other non-binary branches of the trans tree include agender, meaning someone who feels their gender identity is neutral or non-existent, and gender fluid, meaning someone whose gender identity can change over time.

Some trans people may undergo physical procedures such as hormone therapy or surgery to ensure that what they are feeling on the inside matches the outside. However, this is not always the case, and it's important to note that a person isn't defined by the way in which they have transitioned, or if they have chosen to medically transition at all. There is no one way to be trans, and the best way to understand what the trans experience is like is to talk to trans people, and listen to their stories.

In this current political and social climate, our trans siblings are some of the most vulnerable in our community. More and more, we are seeing a tsunami of transphobic rhetoric in our society. Governments across the globe are stripping trans people of their rights, and political figures and bad faith actors are using them as pawns for their own political gain, and attacking a tiny community that wants nothing more than to continue existing as they always have, since the dawn of humanity. We must step up and fight for our trans siblings' rights and inclusion as they have done for us time and time again. Our rights and safety are tied to theirs. Their freedom means our freedom too.

Queer

Queer is a catch-all term for any non-cisgender or non-heterosexual hotties. So, your gender AND your sexuality can be queer. Think of it as a big umbrella (actually more like a gazebo) that you can use to shelter from the heteronormative storm. If you feel like the word suits, then perfect. But you can get more specific if you please. For example, I am queer, but I am also a lesbian. Ta da!

Intersex

Some people confuse transness with being intersex, but my darlings, there you would be mistaken. Intersex people have reproductive anatomy, genes or hormones that don't fit into the typical female/male definition we have for sex. As with trans people, there are many ways to be intersex and there are many different variations of intersex people. Some intersex people can be born with internal 'female' reproductive organs (i.e. ovaries and a womb) but are also born with 'male' genitalia, e.g. a penis. Intersex people are walking, talking proof that gender does not equal biology!

There are countless wonderful combinations of what intersex can look like. Still, the bottom line is that your genitalia is no one's business but your own, and people should concern themselves with respecting how you choose to express your gender identity, not what's between your legs. Hey, governments, I'm talking to you!

Asexual/aromantic (ace/aro)

If you're asexual, then that means you experience little or no sexual attraction to other people. Aromantic means you have little or no romantic attraction to others, or desire for romantic affection. Asexual people can definitely still fall in love, but aren't that interested in bumping uglies. For my aromantic hotties, sensuality, sexuality and sexual satisfaction may take centre stage, without the desire for a romantic connection. The difference between sexual and romantic attraction is complicated and depends on the person, so some people may use these terms differently to others, depending on how they feel they apply.

+

What the hell does 'plus' mean? Dear reader, this is the big etcetera. Basically, it's an inclusion of everything that hasn't been explicitly covered by the previous letters. Think of it as another catch-all for the hotties outside the heterosexual, cisgender sphere, including those who are #anti-label.

If I were to name all the sexual identities, we'd be here till Pride 3026! So here are a few of the more common identities not covered by the rainbow acronym.

Pansexual: If you're thinking that pansexual and bisexual are the same thing, then you'd be close, but not quite right. A lot of people use the terms interchangeably, but when it comes to the strict definition of pan, this is usually said to refer to an attraction to people *regardless* of their gender.

Demisexual: Do you have extremely high standards, or are you just demisexual? Demisexual means that you are only sexually attracted to someone after you form an emotional bond with them. This one's for the divas who can't fathom a one-night stand.

Pomosexual: And if none of the above are feeling right, then maybe you're pomosexual. Pomosexual means that you refuse, avoid or don't feel like you truly align with any of the other labels.

FLINTA*

Congratulations! You've nailed the LGBTQIA+ acronym and have officially graduated to FLINTA*. We queer people clearly love an acronym, so here is another one that will be easy to understand now that you have successfully passed the first level of your training. FLINTA* means Female, Lesbian, Intersex, Non-binary, Trans, Agender and *. This acronym originated in Germany and is used to describe anyone who is not a cisgender man and, therefore, is excluded from and oppressed by the patriarchal society we unfortunately live in. The * acts the same as the +, including any other additional outliers from marginalised genders. Social events and groups will often label themselves as 'FLINTA only' to provide safer and more inclusive spaces for such groups.

RECLAIMED LABELS

'When you say "that's so gay", do you realise what you say?'

The term 'queer' technically means 'strange', and has been used to ostracise the community as far back as 1865, when it was used as an insult against fellow gay author Oscar Wilde. Over one hundred years later, the word got a new lease of life during the AIDS crisis, with the chant that I've since shouted at many a march: 'We're here and we're queer!' To many older LGBTQIA+ people, the word still carries the weight of the homophobia it once signified, and they tend to avoid using it. I find that my grandma flinches whenever I describe myself or my sisters as queer, as she still sees it as the slur it was during her youth, rather than the term of empowerment and defiance it is today.

When I was growing up, the word 'gay' was used similarly, even, admittedly, by me. Something that was cringe, ugly or bad was automatically deemed gay. 'Ew, that's so gay' was a phrase thrown around a lot at school. Today, using gay as an insult is a big no-no, and we, of course, have Hilary Duff's unforgettable anti-homophobia campaign to thank for this. Thanks, Hilary!

Gay, queer, dyke and many more such words were, for a long time, considered slurs. Many people, including yours truly, have reclaimed these labels, finding power in using them to describe themselves and to remove the stigma or shame that others were attempting to inflict. Now, we wear them as badges of honour, or rather as rings on our fingers. Sticks and stones...

With reclaimed labels, there is not a one-size-fits-all approach, but a general rule of thumb is that if the word applies to you and it feels good, then darling, say it loud! If the word was never used to insult your gender or sexual identity, then shut it, boots!

CHANGING YOUR OWN DEFINITIONS

Once upon a time, I was bisexual. Gasp! I know. It might also shock you to know that I once identified with the goth community as well. This is all to say that labels aren't permanent if you don't want them to be. When figuring out who you are or what you like, your label can reflect what you feel in the moment.

Now, this doesn't mean that everyone's sexuality is fluid. Many lesbians, myself included, have been victims of straight men claiming we 'just haven't had the right dick yet' and that they can change us, which is absolutely not the case.

The point is, changing labels shouldn't provoke shame as it so often does, but rather demonstrate the empowerment of discovering more about yourself. Think of these labels as for you, as opposed to for other people. Try them on, see what fits. Maybe none do – outliers exist in all aspects of nature – and in that case, labels shmabels!

CHAPTER 4

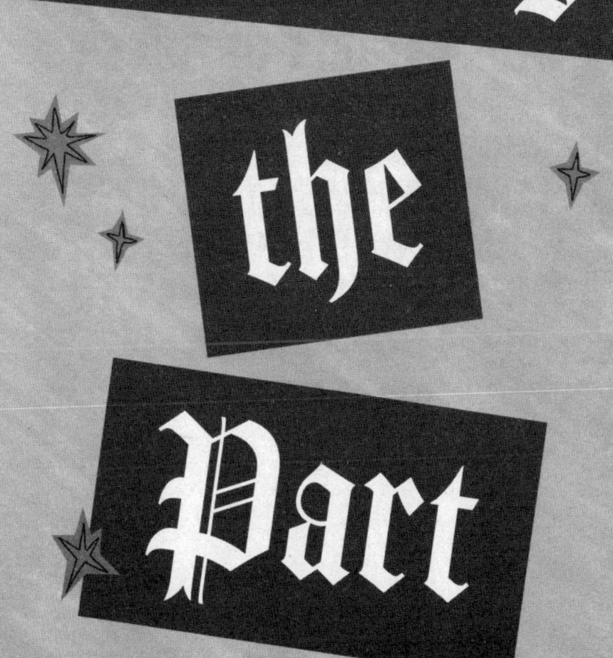

Looking the Part

SAPPHIC FASHION EXISTS AS AN EXPANSIVE LOOKBOOK EXHIBITING A WIDE VARIETY OF QUEER DRESS. FROM STRICT ARCHETYPES SUCH AS HARD FEMMES TO LOOSE CHIMAERAS LIKE FUTCH, THERE IS NO ONE WAY TO LOOK QUEER.

Now that we've covered all the essentials to get you talking like a dyke, I'm sure you're itching to get walking like one, too. But wait, before you rush to pick up the razor and carve yourself a soft-masc mullet, or splash out on a pair of second-hand Docs, let's break down the lore behind the so-called dyke uniform, and give you all the essentials to start building your own capsule wardrobe.

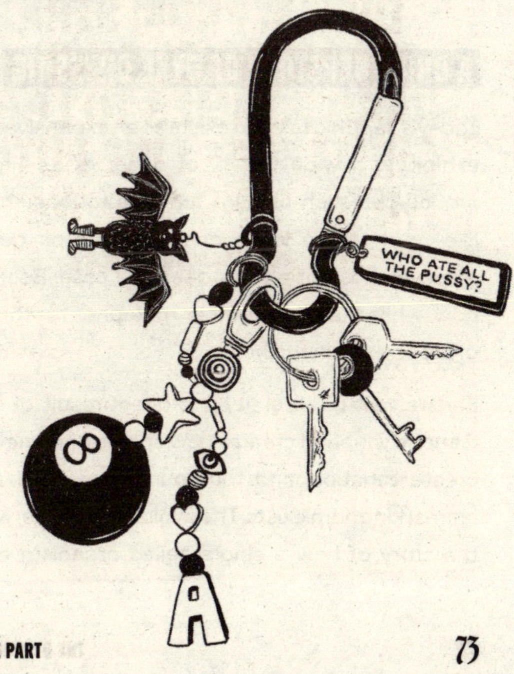

Our identity is woven into the fabric of what we wear, and anything worn on the backs of queer people is inherently political. For as long as queer people have existed – so, since the dawn of time (it was Adam, Eve AND Steve remember!) – we have been opposing societal norms and expectations. It's important to understand that a longstanding sartorial herstory underpins our radical existence through identity and expression. Without all those brave lesbians who donned their dyke uniform in much more adverse times, we wouldn't have nearly as much freedom to present however we choose today.

So pick up a pencil, darlings, because class is about to begin.

A BRIEF HERSTORY OF DYKE DRESSING

Today's sapphic fashion exists as an expansive lookbook exhibiting a wide variety of queer dress. From strict archetypes such as hard femmes to loose chimaeras like futch, there is no one way to look queer. This, however, has not always been the case. Bear with me now, while I use yet another metaphor for the creation of life to explain further...

Earth's vast biodiversity is a direct result of evolution. Genetic variation creates new species, and new species create variation, and thus our diverse and abundant animal kingdom exists. The evolutionary tree, which tells the story of how a single-celled organism eventually evolved into today's walking, talking human, also bears billions of branches for other species created along the way that also still exist today.

This Darwinian-style theory can also be used to describe the evolution of dyke dress. Once the picture of a lesbian was just a woman wearing all black and rocking a cane, but our dykeological evolution means that there are now golden retriever pocket mascs, lululesbian femmes and everything in between (see page 34 for more on queer terminology). As one iteration of what a lesbian looks like becomes a staple, two new ones grow, like a giant jort-wearing homo hydra.

So, here is a brief (pun intended) breakdown of dyke fashion history. The mother of this topic is undoubtedly the brilliant Eleanor Medhurst, and her fascinating book *Unsuitable: A History of Lesbian Fashion* is the source for most of the information in this chapter. I cover just the tip of the iceberg, so if this gives you the urge to learn more, then you simply must run to your local bookshop and pick up Eleanor's book (after you've finished this one, of course).

It's no surprise to anyone that the poster boy (or poster dyke If you're nasty) of lesbian fashion more often than not depicts a more masculine-presenting woman, but why is this? At least in part, this is because historically, dressing masculine would allow lesbians to go about their lesbianism without raising eyebrows. Working-class lesbian couples in the eighteenth and nineteenth centuries would often get married in the guise of a heterosexual couple, with one partner dressing as a man. These cross-dressing dykes would live their life as men to circumvent heteronormative societal pressures, meaning that they could earn a living and spend a happy life flying under the gaydar as hetties when they were, in fact, scissor sisters.

Of course, there is a high chance that some of these dykes were actually trans men and were living their lives as their true gender. Remember that this was ye olden days. These stories have been documented through the lens of the time, which does not account for the nuances of gender and sexuality that we understand today. Now we know that for some people, dressing masculine is affirming their gender, whereas for others it affirms their sexuality.

Anne Lister (1791–1840), an aristocratic Yorkshirewoman famous for her diaries, is often thought of as the 'first modern lesbian'. She appropriated men's dress for her own self-expression, while never claiming to be a man, and married a woman also named Ann. Anne and Ann walked so Rose and Rosie could run. We know so much about Anne Lister because she kept extensive diaries written in a code she invented called 'crypthand', a cocktail of Greek letters, algebraic symbols, punctuation and (like a good lesbian) zodiac signs. RIP Anne Lister, you would have loved Co-Star. Lister was often called 'Gentleman Jack' by her male peers, who mocked her for her gentlemanly attire and manners. She adopted typically masculine sartorial features, such as carrying a cane, wearing braces and waistcoats, and dressing only in black. At this time, upper-class women were expected to wear colour, so Lister's all-black uniform was a symbol of her rejection of society's understanding of modern femininity and heteronormativity.

By the 1920s, there had been a boom in masculine fashion in the mainstream. The interwar period saw women rejecting traditional and restrictive clothes for looks that exuded modernity and rebellion, something lesbians had done for years. High-society, trendy women leaned into the boyish look, rocking cropped hair, tailored clothing, and often a monocle, which had been adopted from aristocratic men. One of the reasons 1920s lesbian fashion was *en vogue* was because lesbians were actually in *Vogue*. British *Vogue* had two dykons running the show, with sapphic power couple Dorothy Todd and Madge Garland as the editor-in-chief and fashion editor of the celebrated magazine, respectively. Their queer influence trickled down into the mainstream fashion scene as Vogue dictated the trends of the time.

These fashions were not outwardly labelled queer, of course, so no one knew that the masculine dress they were sporting was subculturally lezza. This was the case up until 1928, when dyke author Radclyffe Hall released the controversial book *The Well of Loneliness*, which

VOGUE
Late March 1926
One Shilling

exposed the notion that dressing masculine was lesbian AF. The book was the first time that knowledge of underground lesbian fashion and culture was available to the mainstream. Naturally, women's fashion rapidly swung away from masculine sartorial features. Who would want to be mistaken for dressing like a lesbian? Ew! The book was soon taken to trial for obscenity and banned, with all existing copies destroyed because of its lesbian depictions. Classic.

This didn't stop lesbians from rocking the look, though, with the best examples in 1930s Paris, the decade that really put the gay in *Le Gay Paris*. The city had gained a reputation for its night-time hedonism, and with the city's laissez-faire attitude, many gay and lesbian nightclubs were flourishing. Le Monocle, credited as being one of the first lesbian bars, was definitely the most famous. At its peak, the club in Montmartre was considered luxurious, with long queues and an all-female orchestra. It was known as a fashionable and safe place for women to dance, talk and smooch without judgement or persecution. Inside, you would find sapphics in dresses or full tuxedos, hair slicked back and short in a trendy style known as the Eton crop, or in fuck-ass bobs. Goers donned specifically sapphic accessories of the time, which might include a pinky ring, a white carnation or violets (a flower associated with Sappho) pinned to their jacket lapel, or a spunky little monocle, the bar's namesake. There are some incredible pictures taken inside the bar that absolutely warrant a quick google.

By the end of the 1930s, the world had descended into yet another war, and the need for increased military meant there was a major campaign to recruit women into the workforce. This Girl Can! Although homosexuality in the military had been a big no-no as far back as the eighteenth century, the screening for gay men was a lot stricter than for gay women. Strong, masculine women who could perform men's jobs were a much-needed resource during wartime. Many butch dykes joined up and thrived. Masculine garments were more practical than feminine clothing for these jobs, and thus began the long journey of the boot in the dyke uniform hall of fame.

After World War Two, a moral panic swept the US, dubbed the 'Lavender Scare'. It sounds quite cunty, but not for us queers! The general consensus was that homosexuals were perverts and posed a threat to national security if in the workplace, as they were more susceptible to communist blackmail. Talk about clutching at straws. Queer people who presented queer were at risk of losing their jobs, and butch women weren't able to work 'women's jobs' like teachers or secretaries. Many butch dykes worked blue-collar jobs instead, donning the clothing associated with the labour force. Picture flannel shirts, heavy work boots, work trousers and drum roll... carabiners!

Around this time, from the 1940s through the 60s, police in New York and other American cities enforced the 'three-piece law'. This rule meant you could be arrested if you weren't wearing at least three pieces of clothing for your assigned sex at birth. Rules like this had actually existed from as early as the 1800s in order to 'crack down' on criminals who were supposedly cross-dressing to evade police. But this eventually evolved into a means by which law enforcement could persecute queers. Sound familiar? The gag is, this 'law' wasn't in any actual legislation; instead, it was an informal rule that police officers used to abuse their power and, in turn, queer people. As underwear counted as articles of clothing, many lesbians and trans men were subjected to sexual abuse and harassment. Some would spend the work week in their feminine attire and then, once in the safe space of the underground lesbian bars where they would spend their weekends, would change into their more masculine clothes. These dykes were known as Saturday night butches.

It was in these underground bars that the femme (or fem) and butch archetypes came to full fruition. These places were a haven for working-class queers to be themselves and celebrate community; a safe place where lesbians could dress how they wanted without fear of persecution. Inside, you would find femme dykes in dresses, high heels, cinched waists, and pencil or flared skirts, often with silk blouses and accessories like floral brooches. This was juxtaposed with the butch dykes in sporting jackets, flannel shirts, chinos and, on weekends, men's dress trousers, button-downs and ties.

Black studs and femmes in the 1950s dressed more in line with the culture and fashions of the Black community at the time. This was a more formal attire that wasn't just reserved for weeknights. Think studs in full three-piece suits and men's dress shoes, while femmes sported their highest feminine glamour and beauty.

One style dykon of the 1960s who simply can't go without mention when discussing lesbian fashion history is Stormé DeLarverie. Known as 'the Stonewall Lesbian', she is often credited as having thrown the first punch in the 1969 Stonewall uprising, thus galvanising the crowd to fight back against the police raid of the namesake queer bar. She was a Black butch lesbian known for her dandyish approach to suits and men's tailoring, both on and off the stage, where she performed as a drag king. DeLarverie was also known to rock a badass leather jacket when she worked as a bouncer at queer bars in Greenwich Village, NYC. Self-proclaimed 'guardian of lesbians', DeLarverie would patrol the streets with a concealed rifle in the pocket of her leather jacket, making sure the lesbians and queer kids of New York City were safe from discrimination or 'ugliness', as she called it.

Today, leather jackets are a staple in any dyke's wardrobe, but back then they were worn for both fashion and protection. Not only did they look badass AF, so no one dared start anything, but the thick leather actually acted as an armour from physical violence, which plenty of dykes were accustomed to. Alexa, play 'Leather Jacket' by Thunderbitch.

The 1970s brought second-wave feminism and the lesbian feminist movement, which sought to fight back against heteronormativity and the patriarchy. As such, there was a rejection of the butch/femme dynamic, as some lesbians viewed this as conforming to hetero gender roles, a stance that is largely rejected today.

Utilising ugliness as a tool to free themselves from misogynistic expectations, 1970s sapphics took up an anti-fashion dyke uniform that consisted of button-down work shirts, tank tops, jeans, no bra, often with short, cropped hair, and the now infamously dykey Dr. Martens. This sensible shoe had firmed its place in our wardrobe as early as the 1950s, but powerful pictures of Doc'd up lesbians marching in their masses in the protests of the era cemented them as an inexplicably lesbian shoe.

London in the 1980s was home to the dykonic punk subculture the Rebel Dykes. And yes, they're as cool as they sound. Clad in leather, which was war-painted with sapphic symbols reclaimed by the community, such as the labrys, Sappho's colour purple, and the black triangle, a symbol once used to identify lesbians in Nazi Germany. The Rebel Dykes were the antithesis of how the perfect woman was supposed to present. Pretty and dainty feminine features were replaced with metal piercings, coloured hair and badge-adorned leather jackets. Their ostentatious queer dress stood stark against the homophobic backdrop of Thatcher's London. Section 28 had just been passed: a controversial law prohibiting the intentional promotion of homosexuality by local authorities and councils, adding to an already hostile environment for queers. In the face of adversity, these dykons didn't shy away or conform; instead, they were on the front line in the fight for our rights, Mohawks and motorbikes at the ready.

The 1990s skyrocketed lesbian fashion and culture into the mainstream. Up until this point, people pooh-poohed The Lesbian Look™ as a picture of a woman who was hairy in all the wrong places, stomping all over the place in big dykey boots. Bleugh! But a few magazine covers of one celesbian changed all that. k.d. lang, Canadian singer and certified butch dyke, was the cover star of *New York* magazine. With a smoulder that could melt any sapphic, lang stares straight down the camera lens in a suit and sexy androgynous look. The words 'LESBIAN CHIC' are plastered across the bottom. At this point, lesbians had scarcely been in mainstream print, let alone on the actual cover, and to be labelled as chic?! This was a major PR turn for us lezzas. A couple of months later, lang is on another cover, but this time it's *Vanity Fair*. She is pictured lying back in a barber's chair, rocking a sexy masc waistcoat moment, with shaving cream all down her face and neck. None other than supermodel Cindy Crawford leans over her in a black swimsuit, holding a razor. It's hot, chic and undoubtedly gay AF.

The 1990s and 2000s weren't short on fashion dykon representation. Jenny Shimizu, model and masc dyke, was seen with two of the biggest baddies of all time on her arm: Madonna and Angelina Jolie. Shimizu's short, buzzed hair and low-slung jeans gave her an effortless cool-girl look that is sure to be on every soft masc's Pinterest board today. Bette Porter, although fictional (we take what we can), was serving up serious lesbian chic realness on the TV screen in the groundbreaking lesbian sitcom *The L Word*. Bette's sleek silhouettes and SH-E-O suits were the pinnacle of what the mainstream deemed to be an acceptable image of lesbians. Even household TV shows were peddling this narrative. To quote It Girl Carrie Bradshaw, 'The power lesbian. They seemed to have everything: great shoes, killer eyewear and the secrets to invisible make-up'. Real recognises real.

All of a sudden, the lesbian aesthetic had gone from anti-fashion to the forefront of style and, unlike in the 1920s, there was no hiding that this expression was queer. But while this ever-so-slightly androgynous, not-too-masculine picture of lesbianism may have been popular in the mainstream, it wasn't with many actual lesbians. To be 'lesbian chic', you supposedly had to be wealthy from your girlboss job at the top of an S&P 500 company, or wherever power lesbians worked. How else would you afford all your neutral-toned tailoring? Being skinny and white was also preferable.

This demonstrated a very rigid picture of what a lesbian looked like, and anything that strayed too far was very unchic. It also put a pretty bow on the picture of lesbianism, while ignoring any of the struggle and hardships that being queer brought. Gradually, the accepted picture of a lesbian got more and more feminine, and also more sexualised by men. Yawn. This led to a rise in what was termed 'heteroflexibity', where women were seen to be performatively lesbian in order to get attention from men. Double yawn.

Although this lesbian representation was far from perfect, it was still representation, and for the most part, it was positive. For a group of people who had been excluded from the mainstream for, like, literally ever, it signalled change. The sapphic tide was turning. Finally.

An amalgamation of all those who came before led to the massive explosion of archetypes and representation we have today. The Big Bang vibes. That's three for three creation metaphors by the way, if anyone's keeping track.

In today's fashion world, queer women dominate. Leading the charge are the likes of Chappell Roan, Doechii, kwn, Billie Eilish, Cat Burns, Lady Gaga, 070 Shake, Janelle Monáe, Nxdia, Towa Bird, to name but a few. At the same time, dykonic fashion moments in media give us endless Halloween inspo: see *Love Lies Bleeding, A League of Their Own, Orange Is the New Black* and every single one of Chappell Roan's music videos. We are being fed after years of fighting for crumbs, and it feels fucking amazing. And we would be nowhere without the dykons who, in a time when standing out risked persecution or even death, utilised fashion as a weapon to fight against heteronormativity and patriarchal gender roles, rejecting expectations in spite of the repercussions. We would have to move through the world very differently. I wouldn't have been able to wear boots and a bikini on national television, that's for sure.

FORGOTTEN FEMMES

As you are now well aware, the dyke uniform has a long and important sartorial herstory that has paved the way for us to be so openly queer with the way we dress. However, you may have noticed that this 'queer dress' is more often than not denoted by how masculine one dresses. For many sapphics, myself included, who want to present more feminine, this can create a tumultuous dynamic.

On paper, I didn't 'look gay', something people (mostly straight men) felt the need to tell me every single time I mentioned it, as if I were a con artist who'd duped them. Like many of my fellow femmes, I was suffering a chronic case of femme invisibility. On top of this, I was famously femme 4 femme, which in this dykeconomy, is a rarer breed. According to my findings, most femmes were into mascs. So, not only was I invisible to my fellow queers, but the femmes I was looking for were also invisible to me, and on the rare occasion I did manage to hunt one down, they would proceed to tell me they preferred mascs. I developed a serious complex. I truly felt like I was in competition with every masc out there, including my best friend, Eliza. Her boxy fits, extensive hat collection and masc silhouette had femmes fighting tooth and nail for a look in. My complex deepened.

One time after a sexy sleepover with a femme, the doorbell went, and I grabbed the first items of clothing I saw so as to not flash the postman. As I re-entered the bedroom in baggy basketball shorts and an oversized shirt *à la* Dad's wardrobe, I was met with vocal and overwhelming adoration for how sexy I looked: that I'd 'never looked better'. My suspicions were confirmed. From that moment on, I vowed to rock my most masc fits on our subsequent dates, fearing that any inch of femininity might send her running. As you probably guessed, there weren't many more dates, as she clearly wasn't the one for me. Post-frontal lobe development, I have managed to shake the idea that it's Amy vs every masc ever, as the person who is right for you will love you regardless of how you choose to present.

It is easy to get carried away with the notion that to 'dress queer is to dress more masculine', as it has been for much of history. Femmes, despite always being there, have often been left out of the big lezzy picture, with our context only read as queer when seen with a masc.

We do not stand out as much as our more masculine-presenting sisters for obvious reasons, and are therefore less documented in the history books. However, this doesn't make us any less queer. We don these clothes, which adhere to the patriarchal standards of heteronormative society, on a body that opposes them. What's queerer than that? I am reminded of a quote I read in Eleanor Medhurst's book *Unsuitable: A History of Lesbian Fashion,* from Black femme lesbian author Jewelle L. Gomez's work: 'We are in a war for liberation – butches are the front-line troops and femmes are the tactical guerrillas.' Where our masc counterparts fight for our rights with their more obvious rejection of societal norms and expectations, femmes do so in camouflage, behind enemy lines. On the surface, we appear to submit to traditional norms, but beneath the surface, we subvert them. It is blasphemous, radical and ostentatiously queer.

STEREOTYPES AND SIGNIFIERS

Now, there are some sartorial elements that are undoubtedly dykey AF, but aren't specifically masculine or feminine. These are great tools to hint at one's dykonic disposition without having to sacrifice one's preferred gender expression. For example, a carabiner is a classic telltale sign someone is sapphic, but how you wear it is up to you. Mascs may clip a carabiner to their belt loop, but a femme might rock a pink carabiner earring.

Hands are a great starting place for anyone wanting to ham up their sapphic identifiers, as the rule of thumb (and finger) is that they're inherently dykey. Mascs showing off their hands was a big trend on TikTok for a while, and in the Chinese WLW community, hands are even considered a lesbian's second face, with many Chinese sapphics prioritising hand care over facials. Looking at people's nails will tell you a lot. If they're short, well, either they have a nail-biting problem, or you're in business. A femme-icure can be a fun way of fighting femme invisibility. This is where you keep the nails on your middle and ring finger short. Form and function, darling!

Of course, there is also the ring theory, which suggests that the more rings on the finger, the higher the chance they munch box (Harvard, 2016). My housemate just reminded me of the 'bitch fit' I had on the London underground when I realised I'd left the house without my rings on: 'How will anyone know I'm gay?' This link between rings and WLWs isn't a new phenomenon. In the seventeenth and eighteenth centuries, a lack of wedding ring could be an indication of your lack of desire to marry a man (because you bat for the other team). From the 1920s through to the 1950s and 1960s, a pinky ring was a common symbol worn by those in the community, particularly butch lezzas. Thumb rings had a major moment in the 2010s – thank you K Stew! Today, dykes also have the option to don DYKE rings *à la* yours truly, which leaves no questions around one's sexuality, and is a surefire way to wink (or rather scream) one's queerness. It is also an element that is free from potential co-option by the straights (more on that later).

Sartorial signals have a longstanding history in the queer community, as this was a way in which queers could subtly flag to others when in unsafe environments that they're cut from the same rainbow cloth. In the 1940s and 1950s in Buffalo, New York, it was common for lesbians to get a nautical star tattoo on their wrist to clue others in to their dykehood. This could be easily covered with a wrist-watch if needed, so as not to attract unwanted attention. Sappho wrote poems about violets and lavender as expressions of her love for women, and, as such, these

flowers and the colour purple are among the oldest Sapphic symbols. In the 1920s, a sprig of lavender pinned to the lapel was a good indication that someone was lezza. Sapphic semiotics also have a history of flagging an individual's sexual proclivities. A carabiner clipped to one's belt is a sign of general fruitiness, but could also indicate sexual preference. Clipped to the left means a top, and on the right, well, she's a bottom!

Through this flagging system, queers could foster community in a world that persecuted them, by knowing who it was safe to be themselves around. Back then, these symbols had to be both subtle to outside eyes but super obvious to those in the know. While flagging still exists, it does not hold the same weight or importance in most of the Western world today. Our queer elders fought for our rights and our visibility, and as such we do not have to use a secret language to flag our existence. Many of us are lucky enough to feel comfortable being visibly queer, declaring ourselves loudly through our clothes, haircuts and accessories.

CO-OPTION BY STRAIGHTS

Ironically, the pendulum has now swung so far the other way that dressing dykey AF is actually super fashionable. All the straight fashion It Girls seem to have adopted more masculine styles, with jorts, boots, ties and suits seen on the likes of Bella Hadid, Kendall Jenner and Emma Chamberlain, to name but a few. As is often the case with subcultures shunned by wider society, the mainstream culture has eventually come around to deeming the countercultural aesthetic of it all to be actually cunty boots, and has co-opted it. While this assessment would, of course, be correct, it is frustrating to know that the group of people that for so long persecuted us for donning these very clothes are now rocking them without fear of consequence, or acknowledgement of the battles that queers faced in doing so.

More and more often, while walking the streets of east London, I find myself asking the question: 'Are they queer or do they just have impeccable style?' It is difficult to tell who exactly is for the girls these days, as straight women don jorts, Dr. Martens, and even have carabiners hanging off their belt loops. It was already challenging enough looking for a lover as a queer fish in a hetero sea. But now, with queer fashion becoming mainstream, spotting a potential mate, or even someone to discuss Bechloe ship theories with, has become exponentially more difficult. Where once subtle signifiers allowed us to spot each other in a crowd, said signifiers now act as camouflage, blending us into the masses.

As such, we are left to get more creative with the ways in which we can express our queerness and stand out from the hetero crowd. One way in which I do this is by wearing a baby tee that says 'Who ate all the pussy?' while holding hands with my girlfriend in public, and letting our DYKE rings clang together in a sweet sapphic symphony. Works a treat!

TIMELINE OF DYKE DRESSING

1800s

Anne Lister the 'first modern lesbian' dressed in all black with a top hat and cane, which were considered manly sartorial features.

1920s

Sapphic power couple Dorothy Todd (right) and Madge Garland (left) were the editor-in-chief and fashion editor of *Vogue*.

1930s

Patrons of Le Monocle often sported an Eton crop, pinky ring, a white carnation pinned to their lapel and, of course, the eponymous monocle.

1940s

Wartime dykes donned masculine garments for practicality.

1950s

Femme and butch archetypes come into fruition.

1960s

Stormé DeLarverie. known as 'the Stonewall Lesbian', is often credited as having thrown the first punch in the 1969 Stonewall uprising.

1970s

Queer women utilising ugliness as a tool to free themselves from misogynistic expectations led to an unofficial dyke uniform.

1980s

Rebel Dykes were the antithesis of how the perfect woman was supposed to present.

1990s

The sleek silhouettes and SH-E-O suits of the era become fashion forward and labelled 'lesbian chic'.

2000-now

The modern dyke must now wear not-so-subtle signifiers as the The Lesbian Look™ goes mainstream and is co-opted by the straights.

CHAPTER 5

Dating

HOW DOTH ONE FIND A FELLOW WULUHWUH? IS IT BY FIDDLING WITH YOUR SEPTUM RING AT A GAY BAR? GOING TO A RENEÉ RAPP CONCERT AND WAVING YOUR RING-ADORNED HANDS IN THE AIR, FRESH FEMME-ICURE AND ALL?

If you've made it this far into the book, I feel like we've established that even a tiny part of you is #poof4foof. While that's absolutely fantastic, it's time for less talk and more action. Diving into the dyke dating pool is the next big step, which can understandably be intimidating for a baby sapphic... I should know. I spent much of my university experience pining after girls with no real intention of pursuing them. Why? Because that's scary and girls are hot, duh! Had my now-ex not made a pass at me after going through my Instagram following and seeing that I followed a suspiciously large number of lesbian YouTubers (guilty as charged!), I'd probably still be stuck yearning after girls from the sidelines. Don't get me wrong, I'm a slut for a good yearn – I am a dyke after all – but at some point, you do just have to spread your wings and sample the sapphic buffet. TRUST ME.

Unfortunately, not everyone can be so lucky as to have someone push them (somewhat involuntarily) into the dyke dating pool. Others will have to jump in themselves. For some brave souls, this will be easy, and they will have no trouble swan-diving in. But for those like me, who are easily overwhelmed by the thought of getting a little bit wet, it's best to start by dipping in a toe. Don't you worry, though, I will have you fully submerged and ready to swim by the end of this chapter.

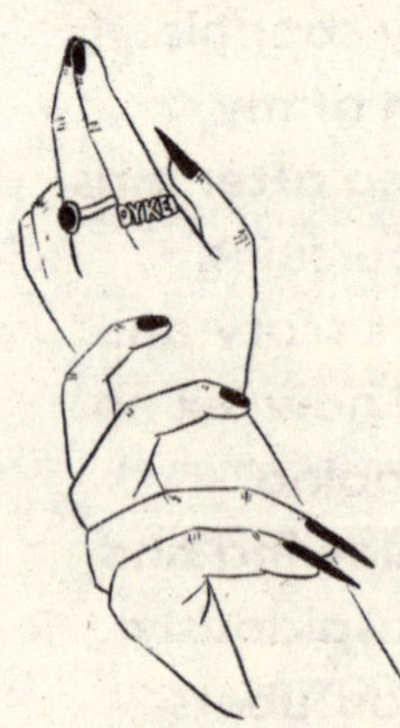

HUNTING SEASON

How doth one find a fellow wuluhwuh? Is it by fiddling with your septum ring at a gay bar? Going to a Reneé Rapp concert and waving your ring-adorned hands in the air, fresh femme-icure and all? Or what if you tried running around Soho with all your carabiners clanging loudly like a modern-day town crier, alerting any nearby dykes that you're DTS (down to scissor).

The modern sapphic has a wide array of options for finding potential lovers, whether that be IRL or online. Now that you've got the The Lesbian Look™, maybe you feel confident and sexy enough to approach potential love interests when you're out in the wild. Sometimes, it can be hard to tell if they, too, are #poof4foof, so I've curated a little list of questions for you to ask them if they haven't mentioned their ex-girlfriend in the first five minutes of meeting, or if you can't tell if their jeans are baggy in a fashionable way, or in a spend-their-weekends-face-deep-in-pussy type of way.

* **'Do you listen to girl in red?'**
* **'Do you own, or have aspirations to own, a Subaru?'**
* **Flippantly mention Villanelle from *Killing Eve*. Do they start panting?**
* **'Do you know your time and place of birth?'**
* **'Who is your favourite character from *Orange is the New Black?*' A trick question because any answer is gay AF.**
* **'Do you have any interest in, or desire to, munch box? Perhaps, potentially, maybe even mine?'**

If this feels a little daunting, and you are more of an introverted type, you could try your hand at swiping on the apps. Everyone knows that dating apps are malevolent forces conjured from the very depths of hell... but there are some benefits. For example, flirting from the comfort of your couch while twirling your bush and watching *The Hunting Wives* for the fifth time. Meeting on an app also instantly places you in a romantic context, so you don't have to pull out your hair decoding whether they asked to hang out because they liked your *vibe*, or because they liked your vibe, if you know what I mean.

And hey, if none of the above options work, you can always try being set up in a masseria by Cupid (Dannii Minogue) and kissing your match upon first meet under the blazing Italian sun. Maybe you'll have better luck than I did...

FRIENDLY OR FLIRTY?

Now comes the next dance, figuring out if it's best buds or bed buds. Sapphic sexual tension is a slippery bugger, and if handled wrong, can easily slide into friendship territory – although famously, that doesn't necessarily mean it's game over in the gay world. Some lesbians aren't opposed to blurring the lines on the odd occasion. But, how does one tell whether it's game on, or if you've just successfully expanded your gay circle by one?

Because this is a safe space, I'm going to tell you a little secret, OK? Come closer. Closer. *Even I still can't figure out when someone is flirting or just being friendly.*

As a serial delusionist who also has the innate habit of constantly doubting herself, reading context clues is something I have always struggled with whenever I'm single.

Is she touching my shoulder in a *Portrait of a Lady on Fire* kinda way, or because there's lint on my coat? Is she maintaining eye contact because she's desperate to finger me, or is it because we're, like, having a conversation? Are we making out because she's planned our wedding in her head or because she sees me as a friend?!

Unfortunately, there is no definitive flashing sign above someone's head saying, 'Yes, I am flirting with you, I think you're sexy and I wanna shag!' The only thing we can control is how we act, or whatever my therapist said. Here are some handy ways to subtly let your potential suitor know you see them in a romantic and not a platonic way, so that you're both on the same page.

* **Be confident, chill and calm. Try using the following template to ask her out: 'Would you maybe like to hang out, on a date, and go get a drink on a date, in a way that is romantic and not platonic, because it is, in fact, a date?'**

* **Ask her if she would like to go to the cinema, and caveat that she should probably clear her schedule for next week as well.**

* Talk for a couple of months online before finding a date that works for both of your busy schedules. Ask her if she would like to get a drink at a sexy, candlelit bar. Get nervous and talk about your ex the whole time. Give her a high five as you leave.
* Message your group chat titled 'Scissor Sisters'. Send the profile of your potential date to get the goss about who has previously dated her. Ask her ex, who is invariably in the chat and also your best friend, for ideas for a nice restaurant to take her to. Plan a romantic evening full of grand gestures, inviting her via carrier pigeon. Ghost her because you have fallen in love with her before the first date and you can't hack the pressure.
* Or, you could simply try asking, 'Can I take you out on a date?'

A WORD OF WARNING

If you take one thing away from this book, let it be this: never fall for a straight girl. I hate to be the bearer of bad news, but we do, unfortunately, live in a society where the rule of thumb is straight until proven otherwise. While the possibility of forbidden fruit does make for a juicier yearn, it also leaves us in the vulnerable position of having our hearts ripped out of our chests, thrown to the floor and stomped on like a cool girl nonchalantly putting out a ciggy. Alexa, play CATTY '4am (Back in His Bed)', Nxdia 'She Likes a Boy', Chappell Roan 'Good Luck, Babe!', Reneé Rapp 'Pretty Girls'... the list goes on. There's a reason so many of our sapphic pop divas write the most gut-wrenching songs about this very topic. Spoiler alert: it never ends well.

Reading into homoerotic tension between you and your home girl is one hell of a drug, and hey, for a while, I was a hardcore addict. But trust me, it is never worth it. No, your straight best friend doesn't fancy you. No amount of basking in delusional limerence will change that. Because, babe, she's straight! Sorry for the tough love, kid, but I wish someone had afforded me the same advice back when I needed to hear it most. Turn off the self-directed mental music video of her realising she's in love with you, and find someone who's actually bent. There's a whole rainbow out there simply begging to be tasted. Go have a lick, girl!

WLW BREAK-UPS

Picture this. You used one of the awesome aforementioned pick-up tricks, landed a date with a hot, fellow WLW, which naturally turned into a five-day sleepover. You fell in love, introduced her to your family (Grandma loves her, of course), moved in together, bought and are raising twin tabby kittens named Cara and Beena. You've started your own little family together, and all feels right in the world. You're going to surprise her for your one monthaversary by getting her name added to your tattoo sleeve, when BOOM! She dumps you. Are you crying? I am.

I could try and explain what your first WLW break-up feels like, but honestly, no earthly words could even come close to describing that exquisite, raw pain. Mine was so bad that my sister had to drop everything and drive six hours to collect me from university, only to be stuck for the six hours back with me in the passenger seat, sobbing so hard I could barely get a full breath in. All while 'Strange' by Celeste played on a loop. Lady in a movie moment! There's a reason why lesbian break-ups have the reputation for being the worst of all. Not that it's a competition, but we all know if it were, we would so win.

Not knowing whether or not you will actually survive the break-up is all part of the sapphic experience. I think it helps to realise that loving someone so hard that they're etched onto your bones and the mere thought of them leaving tears apart the fabric of your existence, is actually a really beautiful thing and a privilege in itself. If anything, lean into it, watch *Carol*, listen to 'Everything' by MUNA, cry into your vegan Ben & Jerry's and get it all out of your system. Allow yourself to feel it fully before you even begin to think about picking up the pieces. As a seasoned guru, with experience of exactly one (1) break-up, I promise you, you will survive.

I sit typing this at home in east London, while the ex with whom I experienced the break-up to end all break-ups is downstairs in our kitchen, baking cookies with her new girlfriend. To some, the idea of a live-in ex-girlfriend is completely unfathomable (shout out to my straight friends!), but those who are also cliché dykes and understand the dynamic of being besties with your ex, will attest to how truly amazing it is to have them in your life still. I will say this, though: it was not an overnight fix. The golden rule is you! can't! be! friends! straight! away! You need a period of separation, of healing, of not being in love with each other anymore, so then you can come back together to form a friendship.

Luckily for me, I got dumped at exactly the right time in history: March 2020. Somehow, when what I needed most was to be locked away and given time to heal in my mum's arms, I got precisely that. Everyone says you shouldn't shag your ex after you break up, and a nationwide, government-enforced lockdown meant that we couldn't do that even if we wanted to. Which leads me to the most important rule of being besties with your ex: being friends doesn't mean still pinging each other's prawns! A lot of you seem to miss this part...

Despite making it work, I don't fully understand how we got to where we are today. There isn't a world in which I could look at my current girlfriend in a platonic way. Being 'just friends' would crush me, and I wouldn't be able to walk into a room that she was in without feeling very passionate, non-platonic things for her. However, despite knowing I felt the same when I was with my ex, if I ever think about the fact that she and I used to be intimate, I actually dry heave a little (sorry Izzi). I know she feels the same way, and we both find that our relationship is now more reminiscent of siblings. Is that weird?

This stereotype does not apply to all lesbians, though, and the community's opinion on whether it can work is polarised. I once posted a TikTok with my ex, her new girlfriend and my new girlfriend, only to be met with an onslaught of comments saying *'DO NOT NORMALISE THIS'* and others calling us *'toxic positivity, people-pleaser individuals who lack boundaries'.* OUCH!

It's true, everyone's situation differs; some people's exes truly are pricks and should not be touched with a one-hundred-foot barge pole. Don't feel pressured or forced into a situation you aren't comfortable with. If you aren't ready or have no desire to be friends with your ex, don't be made to think you're unreasonable because you're going against the gay grain. However, I disagree with the idea that being friends with your ex puts your new partner in an uncomfortable position. Sorry, not sorry. Trust is the backbone of a relationship; it's down to all parties to respect this and each other. In the same breath, broken trust and related trauma are carried from relationship to relationship, so communication, compassion and understanding are KEY!

THE LESBIAN WEB

Have you heard of the six degrees of separation theory? Basically, it's the idea that two people, no matter how geographically distant, are connected through a chain of no more than six social acquaintances. For example, you know someone whose dad works with someone whose mum's gardener trimmed the bush of a vet who once saved the life of a cat belonging to Taylor Swift. Therefore, you now, in theory, have a not-so-direct link to Taylor and, if so inclined, could pull some strings to put those Gaylor rumours to bed once and for all (or not..?). Well, in Lesbian World we have something similar that links up every sapphic in one beautifully sticky web.

So, what is the lesbian web? Well, I'm so glad you asked! Imagine future you standing in the centre of a circle of every sapphic you've ever kissed, fucked, dated, had a few-years-long-but-never-really-labelled-it-so-are-not-really-sure-if-it-counts-but-it-was-definitely-the-worst-heartbreak-you've-ever-experienced-so-surely-that-counts-for-something fling with, with invisible lines connecting you to each one. Now zoom out. Imagine a line connecting them to every sapphic that they ever kissed, fucked, dated, had a few-years-long-but-never-really-labelled-it-so-are-not-really-sure-if-it-counts-but-it-was-definitely-the-worst-heartbreak-they've-ever-experienced-so-surely-that-counts-for-something fling with. Now think of all the lines that connect them to all their connections and their connections' connections. Then repeat for infinity.

Every sapphic is linked; even you and I, dear reader, are likely connected by this invisible sapphic string theory. You could be dating one of my friend's (whom I've inevitably slept with/kissed/dated) ex-surf instructor's mother-in-law. Or, more excitingly, you could be three situationships away from the likes of Kristen Stewart or even Sarah Paulson. Isn't that beautiful?

The fact of the matter is, there is no getting around the lesbian web. You will date someone that your ex's ex was best friends with. And you will count yourself lucky because that's a looser connection than usual. You are a little ladybird (or non-binarybird) caught up in a big, wide lesbian web. You are entangled, there is no escape, and yes, it will get messy. But babe, that's what keeps the group chat alive!

MEDIA TO CONSUME THROUGH THE DIFFERENT STAGES OF A RELATIONSHIP

Yearning

Read *Sunburn* by Chloe Michelle Howarth. Hard to think of a book that will tug at the heartstrings more.

Making a move

Watch *Bottoms*. This is the baseline amount of work someone should be putting in to make a move on you.

Getting serious

Watch *Glee*. Santana and Brittany's storyline is rare in lesbian representation in that neither of them dies, and although their relationship is not without its bumps in the road, it actually has a happy ending!

Breaking up

Listen to 'Talia' by King Princess. Trust me on this one. Prepare to ugly scream-cry to this (the kind where snot and tears mix).

Post break-up, but still talking

Watch *Killing Eve*. Sometimes you don't even need to date to be exes.

Hating your ex

Read *Fingersmith* by Sarah Waters. Deeply romantic and deeply cruel in equal measure. Think *Gone Girl* but Victorian and gay. By the end you'll have processed about six stages of grief vicariously.

Acceptance

Listen to 'Healing out of Spite' by CATTY. That girl really knows how to go through a break-up. God help whoever's next...

Best friends

The L Word, Bette and Alice. To be fair, you could easily put *The L Word* for any of the above.

CHAPTER 6

LET'S TALK ABOUT DYKE SEX, BABY, OR HOWEVER THAT SALT-N-PEPA SONG GOES...

As a self-proclaimed seasoned professional, I couldn't speak more highly of the practice and will jump on any opportunity to spread the good word, often unprompted. Is this just because I'm a **really** horny dyke? Or am I overcompensating for what now feels like a wasted youth chasing boys? Not because they lit a fire in my loins, but because boys seemed to have that effect on other teenage girls at school and in the media? It's giving sheep. I imagine it's probably a beautiful combination of both. Regardless, Nicole Kidman and I are akin in our advocacy and share the passionate stance that everyone should try lesbian sex at least once in their life. (We've all seen that *Marie Claire* interview right?! Granted she doesn't explicitly mention lesbian sex but if you have an active imagination like me when it comes to context clues, she essentially declares her love for eating pussy.)

For those who wish to partake, *sesbian lex* can be a stupendous way to spend an hour or eight. Sex can bring people closer, not just physically but emotionally as well. It can allow you to feel more intimate with your partner, partners, or even yourself. Some people have to have feelings to have sex; others don't feel the need to conflate the two. Some people have sex to pleasure others, and others have sex to pleasure themselves. Sex can create opportunities for exploration, satisfaction and curiosity.

This is all to say that people have sex for many different kinds of reasons, and whatever your reason may be, there are some things to consider to keep sex sexy. So, before you hop on your Lime bike and cycle down to your nearest independent, queer-owned, sex toy shop to fill your basket up with straps, bullets and lube galore, let's get some basics covered. Whether you've been practising dyke sex for years and are looking for some sexy communication tips, or are entirely new to the craft and want to settle your nerves, this chapter is for you.

WHAT EVEN IS LESBIAN SEX?

One thing I've noticed since being out 'n' proud is the morbid fascination that non-sapphic people have with sapphic sex. A question I used to get a lot from random straight men at uni was 'what even is lesbian sex?' and the answer to that was: none of their business. But if you've picked up this book, we can safely assume it is yours. I'm sure you have clocked that the general rule of thumb when it comes to anything queer-related, whether that be dating, sex, labels etc, is that the heteronormative rules don't apply. This includes the traditional definitions of sex. Doing the deed can involve any sexual activity between you and your romantic partner. That's it. There's no sort of fingering quota you need to hit before it counts as sex. Anything you count, counts! Yes, I did lose my virginity to a girl; no, there was no penis penetration; yes, that still counts. The concept of virginity is so outdated anyway, this isn't an 1980s teen movie about prom night.

While I'm in the habit of coital myth-busting, let me bust another one: scissoring is real. That being said, it isn't for everyone, particularly not those who are faint of hip, which is why it's essential to work out what you enjoy and what you don't. Figuring out what you like in the bedroom (or sofa, kitchen counter, club toilet cubicle...) is a task you should take very seriously. This is your pleasure, goddamnit! Watch (ethical) porn. Experiment. When you're masturbating, think about different things to see what turns you on. Try different toys. Try different toys with different people. Try different people with different toys. Are you aroused by having sex with one person, or is it the more the merrier? Do you prefer external stimulation or internal? Do you like being more dominant, submissive, or switching it up every time?

Don't forget it's not all about what's between your legs. There is an array of erogenous zones at your disposal, ready to be tickled, tribbed, stroked, sucked, licked or whatever you damn well please!

As is the case with all sex practices, what you might like with one partner might not be the same with another, and communication must be prioritised. Talking about what you want can feel scary. Discussing desires, boundaries and expectations can feel so much more vulnerable and embarrassing than just getting naked and boffing. The gag is, to create a safe, sensual and sexy environment, you need to say what you want. In my day-to-day life, I am a die-hard people pleaser and a serial pushover, so asking for what I wanted sexually didn't come naturally to me. It was hard at first, but over time it became easier and more natural. Try using both verbal and nonverbal cues, and don't forget to look out and listen for them as well. This is a shared experience after all!

Lesbian sex does not have the linear narrative that we are taught is the norm in heterosexual sex. Orgasm is not the climax. Having one can equal end of shag, or it can mean that you have reached the first mile in your horizontal marathon. *Sesbian lex* requires a lot of communication and saying what you mean, like *keep touching me here at this pace*, or *let's stop, it's been five hours and I need to feed the cat.*

SAY IT WITH ME: CONSENT IS SEXY

I do not doubt that you understand the importance of consent. Despite knowing this, there is a fear that sometimes it feels clunky to ask, or that it kills the moment. Never fear: this is not the case. Consent is not only necessary, but it is very sexy.

That being said, it can be nerve-racking in the moment and you may end up tripping over your words and saying something really sensual like, *would you mind if I put my hand on your front bum?* That's why I have compiled an easy, handy-dandy list of ways to ask that are not only easy to remember, but also sexy to boot! Feel free to write the following on a Post-it note and stick it above your bed in case of emergency.

* ***Can I kiss you?***
* ***Can I touch you?***
* ***Can I touch you here?***
* ***Would you like me to X your Y?***
* ***Do you want me to do A to B?***

Consent is essential for everyone, and it's important to make people feel comfortable. Touching some people's parts might make them feel alienated or dysphoric, even if they're the same parts of your body that make you feel good. If you're not sure, ask! Ask! Ask!

LET'S PING THAT PRAWN

Once upon a time, I was a baby dyke, one foot out of the closet, barely having kissed a girl. Had a clam presented itself, I wouldn't have had the slightest clue how to joust it. It is so easy to get in your head about doing the deed, especially if it involves parts you've never sampled before. But therein lies the beauty and, like a lot of things, the best way to learn is by doing. First times are always going to be daunting, regardless of the activity. Someone who has jumped out of a plane one hundred times isn't going to be nearly as hesitant as a person doing it for the first time. The unknown can be scary, but that's what makes it fun and exciting.

Yes, sex is sexy, but sex is also funny and weird and messy and hot and fun, and sometimes things won't happen exactly how you planned them. Accidents happen, piercings get caught, rings get lost, periods occur unexpectedly. You might forget to turn the vibrating strap-on off before sucking it and accidentally give your brain a good rattle (a common occurrence, right?). Lesbian sex in particular has all the right tools for a comedy show. There is no sexy way to put on a strap-on, and this is a hill I will die on. But these funny, exposing, awkward moments don't detract from the intimacy; rather, they add to it. Screaming 'DONT LOOK AT ME' while naked and vulnerable, trying to pull up your strap-on harness like you're about to embark on some kinky new zipline, isn't inherently sultry. But from the number of lesbians who love indoor climbing, one can only assume that a sort of Pavlovian response is happening.

Sexy-time mishaps are all part of the sapphic experience and unite us throughout the Dykedom. But don't just take my word for it. I put a call-out on my Instagram story for crazy, sapphic sex stories, and boy, did you guys deliver. If you think you're the only person ever to accidentally kill a girl's goldfish mid-eating them out, then you'd be wrong! Feel free to dog-ear the next few pages for when you need a healthy reminder that shit happens.

'Once, I jumped into bed with a girl a little too eagerly, and caught my nipple piercing on the way in. It bled, I dabbed it up with a tissue and threw it behind me as a joke. Obviously, it caught alight on one of the dozens of candles she had lit to create a vibe. I had to stomp it out with my foot, leaving a burn and wax on the carpet. Needless to say, no sex was had.'

'Got fingered shortly after my partner ate spicy chicken wings. I felt like passing out.'

'I have an IUD, she felt the wire and said, "We've got company." I cried laughing.'

'After a night out, my girlfriend wanted head, but I was so tired I fell asleep halfway through. She didn't want to wake me up, so I woke up dazed and confused in between her legs with my cheek all pruney, like how your fingers get after you've been in the bath for too long.'

'I kept saying "finger me" and she was like, "Why do you keep saying think of me?"'

'I was having a rough go with my girl... We had a glass projector shelf above our bed and when I came up for air I shattered the damn thing all over our naked bodies. We were fine. The wall wasn't.'

'After my first, when I went to get dressed, my flatmate's dog burst in and licked my arse when I bent down.'

'Sprayed blood from my period cup in their face mid-sex obviously.'

'My dick always comes off inside her.'

'Hit my face full force on the headboard mid-orgasm. Think I broke my nose.'

'When I lost my virginity, we had to look up lesbian sex on wikiHow.'

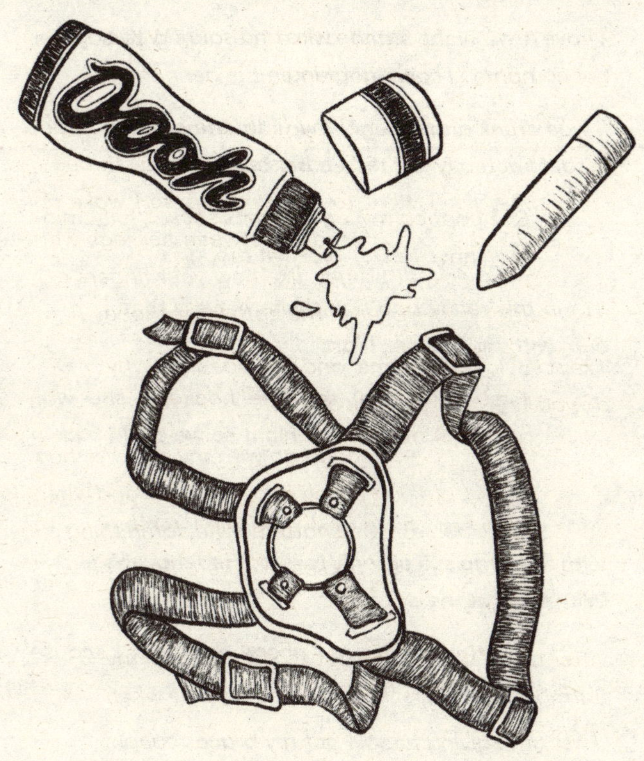

'Lamb vindaloo was embedded under my nail and I didn't know. She had to sit in the tub for hours.'

'Day three of our romance, she fell asleep with her fingers inside of me.'

'Student house. Paper thin walls. Things got heated. Hole in wall. Hello housemate!'

'One night stand asked me during to say her name... I could not remember her name.'

'I was drunk and thought I was squirting, when in fact I actually just pissed her bed.'

'She popped my leg out of its socket, fully, mid-sex (I have hEDS). Worth it though.'

'I'm in this really bad habit where every time I cum with my partner, I fart.'

'First date after multiple hookups, she was biting her nails off all night so we could fuck in the toilets.'

'May or may not have answered the intercom with the strap still on, only to hear the Jehovah's Witnesses at the door.'

'A girl once got her phone torch out because she couldn't find my clit.'

'First time giving head, I got my braces caught on her clit.'

'For some reason I thought it was a good idea to sit on top of an electric hob and we accidentally turned it on and burnt my arse.'

'I got attacked by a spider mid-fingering and jumped off the bed screaming.'

'Started a new job on my birthday this year. To celebrate, I had a nice evening with my girlfriend and got a little bit freaky. Suddenly I hear her yell out, "FUCK, WHERE'S MY RING." Checked my anus, where no ring was to be found. I called the emergency number, they told me to come to A&E urgently. I was at the hospital until 4 a.m. with my girlfriend's mum's wedding ring lodged inside my bowels, which they couldn't find even after a scan. Had to let my boss know the next day – on my second day mind you – why I couldn't come in and, for some reason, when he asked why, I blurted out "sex-related injury". We found her ring next to the sofa that afternoon.'

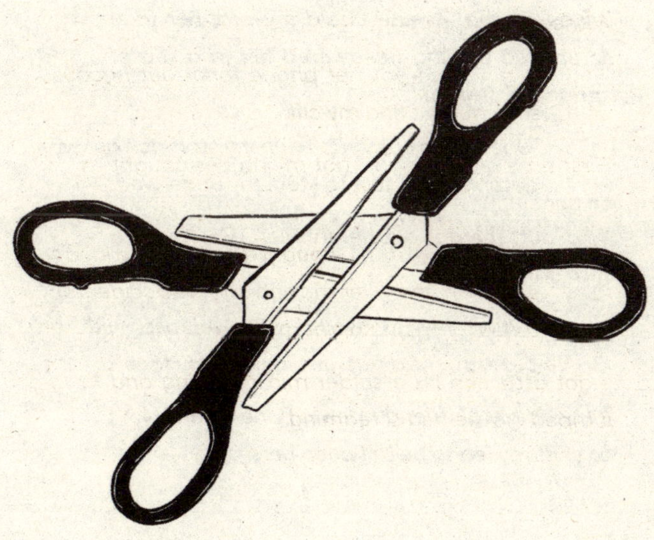

'I, a diabetic lez, took batteries out of my blood sugar sensor to revive a dead vibrator.'

'I was seconds away from starting and she said, "Awww, you just reminded me of my mum. She died a month ago."'

'Was giving her head and accidentally burped into her vagina. It just slipped out.'

'Mid-stroke they said, "Here comes the airplane." Was kind of hard to regain the mood after that, although it did make great fodder for a series of aeronautical-themed jokes.'

'Her actual cat started attacking my foot mid-finger.'

'I was on top. As she undid my bra, her face scrunched up and I showered her in a sea of spring roll crumbs.'

'One time a cat jumped on my stomach as I was getting head, just to steal my underwear.'

'Mid-act, she got out her inhaler. TBH it was a turn on.'

'When my ex would fully release with an orgasm, she'd fart, like, right in my face.'

'I kneed my girlfriend's pelvic bone when trying to shift my leg to be between hers.'

'Oh, one time my girlfriend was giving me head and my cat walked across her ass.'

'My tongue piercing got caught on her clit.'

'My housemate sang that Chappell line LOUD as I was "knee-deep" with my girlfriend for the first time. Divine timing.'

'Pissed myself in her bed from laughing too hard because my gum got stuck in her bush.'

'She knocked a huge, spiky geode that was balanced on the shelf above my bed onto my head while she was sitting on my face. Nearly killed me, so I wrote a song about it lol.'

CHAPTER 7

Comm-

unity

YOU ARE A VILLAGER AND THIS IS YOUR VILLAGE.

I never fully understood the importance of community until I realised what I was missing. Growing up, I had lots of friends, but it wasn't until I found my queer group that I truly felt a sense of belonging.

The whole time I thought I was the only gay in the village... oh, how wrong I was. It turned out I wasn't even the only dyke under my parents' roof. Now my sisters and I are all uncloaked and out of the closet, family Christmases and birthdays are more like a night at a local dyke bar. Combined with our girlfriends we collectively hold the majority, and now family dinner table conversations are debates over who's more queer-coded: Rachel Weisz or Cate Blanchett? I mean, we've all seen that one *Disobedience* scene...

In my second year of university, I met a group of girls through joining a lacrosse society. One by one, each of us slowly came out, and it makes sense to me now why we all flocked to each other in the first place. Our little dyke group flourished as we held each other's hands as we came out to our families, and then helped set up each other's Hinge profiles. My best friend actually met her long-term partner through me. One day at a festival, this short, posh, blonde girl I'd never met before stormed up to me shouting, 'You slept with my ex last night!' Guilty! Next thing I knew, she was necking on with my bestie, and they've been together ever since. Never say I haven't done anything for the community!

Moving to London changed everything for me, with big thanks to my gay friend Rupert, now known as 'the lesbian whisperer'. For some reason, Rupert had loads of sapphic friends who didn't know each other, and he took it upon himself to connect us all. He would throw luncheons and organise pub trips where we could all meet. Our little dyke nucleus would engulf any and all sapphics he put in front of us, much like a phagocyte would cell debris. Hey, Mum, look! I'm finally putting that medical science degree to good use.

Now our group has blossomed, and I'm lucky enough to live with a few of them in London. Our house is known by our local coffee shop as the 'Lesbian Commune', as we are constantly bringing new lesbians from the house to grab a coffee, whether that be our girlfriends, friends, or my sisters and their girlfriends.

Going on *I Kissed a Girl* changed my community even more. Since the show aired, I have been introduced to a whole bunch of new queer people, and my life feels richer with every new addition. I've made sapphic friends online from all over the world, and I've also met some of the most pivotal people leading the charge in the fight for our queer rights. I have never been more proud to be a dyke, and that is because of how much those around me inspire me and add to my life every day. Without dyke community, I would be completely lost.

A HISTORY OF QUEER COMMUNITY

You might wonder why us queers are always harping on about community. Community is the backbone of queer culture. It's safety. It's being understood, seen, known. It's love. It's the reason we can thrive. Culture happens when a community gets together. Community allows us to better understand ourselves and our collective past, and to fight for our collective future.

Throughout our history, persecution has forced us to come together for protection and socialisation, and led us to seek safety in numbers. This is what we call homosocialisation – when groups of people of the same sexual orientation come together to provide a supportive network for each other, and allow a space to affirm identity while counteracting social isolation. For straights, this community is simply called 'society'.

In the 1920s, dyke homosocialisation blossomed in Europe, with many lesbians uprooting their lives and moving to bohemian cities like Paris and Berlin. Bars and clubs like Le Monocle (see page 79) and Damenklub Violetta had vibrant lesbian scenes where queers could meet other sapphics, dance and drink together.

It was a different story over in the US, as Prohibition meant the closure of bars and the shutting down of drinking culture. Instead, lesbians would gather to drink tea in places aptly named 'tea rooms', many of them actually speakeasies that also served alcohol on the sly.

Eve Adams's tea room, also known as Eve's Hangout, was considered one of the hottest spots in the West Village in 1920s New York. In this bar, run by lesbian Jewish immigrant Eve Adams, described as 'queen of the third sex' for her masculine appearance, you would be greeted by a sign that read 'Men are admitted but not welcome'. Need one of those. This place was a safe space where women loving women would come to drink tea, recite poetry and share their experiences without fear of persecution.

Sapphic folk can find community in the most unlikely of places. During World War Two, women's branches of the military were established to free up men for combat. As a result, queer women could escape their straight hellscapes back home and meet people like themselves for the first time. Although technically not allowed, lesbian antics were often overlooked by senior officers, as the need for personnel and manpower was considered far more important. Beggars can't be choosers! Rachel Allen, a World War Two veteran, describes the outbreak of the war as a 'godsend' as she was able to leave behind a string of 'uninteresting boyfriends' by joining the British Auxiliary Territorial Service. There, she encountered queer women for the first time and had her first physical same-sex relationship.

The war was imperative for lesbians and women at large. Even if they did not serve (in the literal sense, not the gay way), the societal disruption allowed women to become skilled and earn their own keep. Having their own money meant women could spend it where they wanted. Enter... dyke bars.

From the 1940s through to the 1960s, dyke bars thrived in the US. Working lesbians found dyke bars to be the perfect place to foster community away from prying, prejudicial eyes. Mona's 440 was one of the first to open in America. Based in San Francisco, this nightclub had the tagline 'Where girls will be boys'. While waiters dressed in white tuxedos, patrons dressed as they pleased and could be their gender fluid, queer selves. Notable drag kings of the time would perform there, including dykon Gladys Bentley, a Black butch lesbian known for her blues sound, and her signature tuxedo and top hat.

Over in London, one lesbian bar stood above the rest. Nestled neatly on the King's Road in Chelsea, the Gateways Club was one of the longest running lesbian clubs of all time, from its opening in the 1930s to its final night in 1985. In its heyday, you would have seen a plethora of celesbians go through its dull green door, including notorious dyke author Radclyffe Hall, her partner Lady Troubridge, and even the likes of musician Dusty Springfield. Supposedly, Mick Jagger once tried to get in, but was turned away because of the strict female-only policy. It is claimed that Mick begged the owner, Gina Ware, to let him in, stating that he'd even throw on a dress. Gateways was a safe place where lesbians could be themselves, and was many women's first introduction to lesbian life.

London's current lesbian ground zero *du jour,* La Camionera, was only meant to be a tapas bar residency in the basement of a bar on Broadway Market, in east London. I didn't personally attend the opening night, but it felt like I may as well have done – my Instagram was awash with stories of every dyke in London trying to get a pint from this one bar. The cobbled streets filled with dykes as they spilled out of the heaving venue, tattooed elbows trying to make any room that they could. The wave of press that followed and the amount of attention the idea received clearly showed that sapphics had a serious craving for a place they could gather and get pissed. La Camionera was able to open a permanent bar in Hackney and now exists as a popular hotspot where WLW can gab over negronis and Perelló olives.

Lesbian bars are and have always been so important because they provide a physical space dedicated to community gathering. Having this space is so crucial because it is a static, unmoving marker of community, reminding people that we exist and we're not going anywhere, even when we aren't physically there.

THE MODERN DYKONOMY

When community is fostered, culture thrives, and this in turn feeds the community. The circle of dyke life. While you can't go wrong with a good dyke bar, it's unfortunately impossible to expect every event to have its own permanent home. Honey, in this economy? Pop-up events offer a more flexible and feasible option for dykes to cultivate the exact community they want, and many of these events are centred around going out. Needless to say, nightlife is inextricably entwined with gay culture. The opportunity to dress up, let loose and dance under the club lights has been a gateway

for many of us to experiment uninhibitedly with our sexuality and our gender expression. Traditionally, many of these spaces have centred cis gay men – but in major cities, such as London, we are definitely seeing a rise in FLINTA*-prioritised events, such as Butch, Please!, Pxssy Palace, U-Haul Dyke Rescue and WET LDN.

While it can sometimes feel like contributing to the dykonomy solely involves sinking pints, it doesn't have to. Don't forget that we are also stereotyped as going on a singular date, U-Hauling, buying a cat, knitting in front of reruns of Ab Fab and falling asleep at a sensible 9 p.m. Now, that's what we call a dykotomy. Luckily, you can also experience dyke life by performing, watching, consuming, talking, experiencing, listening and laughing. There are infinite numbers of lesbian events to discover: comedy nights, cabaret, run clubs, sports teams, theatre, book clubs, supper clubs and concerts.

I have seen first-hand the effects of a community forged through music at my girlfriend Catty's gigs. Queer girls of all ages enjoy her music, and gigs like hers are opportunities for them to come together IRL to support their queer role model. There are cross-generational group chats where they plan things like their outfits, what time they're going to get to the gig, or which song they're most excited to hear. Those who may be going alone are immediately accepted into the fold, and know that it's a safe space for them, too. Seeing these younger and older sapphics come together in a place where they know their queerness is celebrated makes my heart burst with pride and heals something deep in me. Shout out to the Coven!

Going to local queer markets is also a good way to meet and contribute to the community, either by creating dyke art or buying dyke art. If you're in London, the London Dyke Market happens once a year and is an amazing day out, an opportunity to buy sweet gifts and goods, and also a way of directly putting money into the pockets of fellow dykes. Check local listings for similar events in your area.

When it comes to finding community, one of the most obvious and fruitful places to start is sporting communities. I mean, this is where I first found my lezzy kin. Obviously dykes and football go hand in hand,

so by joining a football club in your local area, you are bound to be thrown in with some fellow queers. Not to typecast, but trust me on this one. Recently, my dyke nucleus and I started a five-a-side football team and joined a local league. I'd never played football before, which is evident in the fact I've only ever scored own goals (taking the concept of playing for the other team too literally). The team created an excuse for us to get together every Wednesday, run about, and then catch up on each other's lives over a post-match pint.

If you aren't into team sports, there are still plenty of opportunities to get your body moving while socialising. Dykes Who Hike is the perfect example of this. Originally based in London, this walking group has now expanded across the UK, including Manchester, Norwich, Leeds and Shropshire, and is for queer, bi, lesbian, trans and non-binary folk 'who love a good wander and even better company'. Entwining sports into community building is the perfect way to feed the mind, body and soul.

Finding community within your community is paramount. Intersectionality is key to feeling seen and understood. While I am a dyke, I am white and cis, and therefore my experience of lesbianism will significantly differ to a Black lesbian or a non-binary lesbian with Southeast Asian heritage. Events like WET LDN, a south London dyke night, prioritise Black and POC attendees, ensuring not only that space is held for these members of the community, but also that at these events, importance is placed on these bodies feeling safe and treasured.

MARCHES & PROTESTS

Even before Stonewall, marches and protests have always been a place for the community to gather and fight for our collective rights. Queers, no matter what letter of the acronym, have a long history of standing up for each other. We are only as strong as our weakest member, so when times are particularly tough for one group, it's important that the others take up the mantle and carry our siblings through. Without community and togetherness, this isn't possible. When coming together to demand societal change, protests and marches also naturally become a concentrated gathering of like-minded queer individuals, creating the perfect opportunity to meet new friends and grow your circle.

The London Dyke March is a grassroots, radical march which, after an eleven-year-long hiatus, has returned to the streets of London thanks to Stav B and Shiv Dave – two individuals whom I admire greatly. This anti-corporate, anti-commercial, intersectional event celebrates and amplifies the voices of dykes, sapphic and trans folk alike, while also standing against genocide, bureaucracy, austerity, fascism, war and misogyny. Besides the big day itself, the London

Dyke March creates endless opportunities for the community to come together, whether that be through hosting social events like cabarets and club nights to raise funds and make the march more accessible, or through other activities like group placard-making.

While Pride is probably the most famous march, if I'm being real, these days it's less of a protest and more of an opportunity for partying and corporate pinkwashing. Pinkwashing is where corporations disingenuously show support for LGBTQIA+ communities solely to project a progressive brand image and gain good PR. Behind closed doors, these companies engage in harmful workplace practices and/or support institutions that violate human rights. Pride does still serve as an accessible starting point for people to show up for each other, build community and meet other queer individuals. It is important, however, to stay critical of events like these, which corporations often hijack for good press and profit.

Unfortunately, right now it seems there are endless reasons to get up and protest. Something this special is worth fighting to protect. I'll see you there.

ONLINE CONNECTION

In-person community is obviously vital, but finding your internet community can be an incredible supplement if any of the aforementioned avenues is not available to you. Online community, found on chat rooms, Reddit, Tumblr, YouTube, TikTok, Discord, Instagram and so on, is so important for queers who may not be out or do not live in a major city. Even queers who do live in major cities can access online specific communities that they don't have in real life, allowing them to explore different facets of their queerness and identity. While in-person connection is still wildly important, this access to different niches and exact intersections serves as a digital bridge, linking queers across the globe.

Lesbian Tumblr was that girl back in the day. Famously, it's how OG lesbian YouTuber couple Shannon Beveridge and Cammie Scott first met. They fell in love on Tumblr and, in true lesbian fashion, proceeded to have a long-distance relationship for three years before moving in together. A journey my sister and I were so parasocially invested in that we actually cried in each other's arms when they broke up. The closet couldn't have been more see-through. I personally didn't use Tumblr for socialising, and instead spent most of my time on the platform doom-scrolling Jennifer Lawrence content, who was my secret lesbian fixation back in 2012. Ugh, you just had to be there.

TO HAVE A VILLAGE, YOU MUST BE A VILLAGER

There's this quote that my friends and I say when we're being lazy and can't be bothered to go out of our way for one another. You're rocking a major hangover, but it's your best friend's birthday an hour from where you live. *Inconvenience is the price of community.* When both me and my girlfriend can't be bothered to strap. *Inconvenience is the price of community.* When my friend wants to go on a date with someone I kind-of dated three years ago. *Inconvenience is the price of community.* We're joking, but it's true. Community isn't a passive act. It requires work and dedication, but the reward is beyond worth it.

Sophie Ward, who runs London's queer rodeo night Bonanza, said that one of the main reasons she started it was because she and her girlfriend wanted to make more sapphic friends. 'We'd always see queer couples walking down the street, but didn't know any of them!' A few years later, and the community Bonanza has fostered is beyond anything she could have imagined. 'On an average month, around two hundred cowbabes ride into our north and south London saloons, with lots of returning visitors and familiar faces.' Sophie says that on a personal level, she and her girlfriend have made a whole new group of friends through this queer rodeo, and that there have also been at least five long-term romantic relationships born out of Bonanza.

If you're lacking a specific community experience, this is your sign to make it happen yourself. I'm sure if you've found a gap in the muff market, there'll be others with an appetite for it too. Start that lesbian horror book club, that pansexual pottery workshop or that tap dancing troupe for tribades. Trust me, this is what it's all about.

CHAPTER 8

Advice from Queer Elders

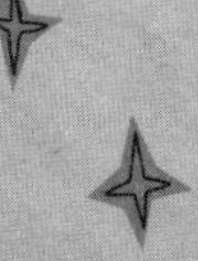

THIS IS NOT OUR FIRST FIGHT. THIS WON'T BE OUR LAST. AS ALWAYS, WHEN FACED WITH ADVERSITY, COMMUNITY IS THE FIRST PLACE TO WHICH WE SHOULD TURN. WE NEED TO WORK TOGETHER, TO LOOK TO OUR ELDERS, TO LEAN ON EACH OTHER, TO LEARN NOT ONLY HOW TO SURVIVE, BUT HOW TO THRIVE.

Since I started writing this book in early 2025, there has been a tangible shift politically across the globe, and I'd be lying if I said I wasn't scared. Daily, my phone screen lights up with a new headline about another way in which queer rights are being attacked. Western politicians are arming themselves with harmful homophobic narratives as their weapons of choice when galvanising the far right.

Not to be bleak, but it just doesn't stack up with me that we're truly in a lesbian take-over if we're simultaneously experiencing a worldwide walk-back on trans and queer rights. This is obviously devastating for us queers, but also for society as a whole. No one is made safer by another's human rights being removed. The spewing of prejudice, intolerance and hatred will only divide us more.

This is not our first fight. This won't be our last. As always, when faced with adversity, community is the first place to which we should turn. We need to work together, to look to our elders, to lean on each other, to learn not only how to survive, but how to thrive.

So I called in some queer elders I look up to, and asked if I could pick their brains. What advice would they give their younger selves? What would they want to make sure they knew, and, by extension, what should we know?

Joelle Taylor, an award-winning poet, playwright and writer, grew up in the late 1970s and 1980s, when homophobia was 'considered the natural state of being' and it was a 'difficult time to be a woman, let alone a lesbian'. Within the shrinking walls of the prevailing misogynistic culture, she found that fostering community was the way forward. 'We fought back by holding hands: we networked, we shared resources and ideas, we built event spaces in bedrooms, we marched, we learned trades from one another, we workshopped, we founded magazines and club nights; we lived.'

Joelle's advice for the next generation is simple: 'Find a way forward as one expansive community, a community that focuses on building rather than demolishing, that thinks about creation over policing of our differences, that holds each of us like a warm egg in a palm.'

Raga D'silva is a speaker, author, podcaster and LGBTQ+ activist who came out publicly when she was nearly fifty. 'It was one of the most freeing moments of my life, but it also came with sadness for the years lost, spent worrying about what people would think. Living authentically finally allowed me to claim my truth and my joy.' Being queer and Indian, she felt the heavy weight of cultural expectations and the shame and guilt that came with that.

Like Joelle, she found that turning to community is the umbilical cord that guides and sustains us all. 'We must listen to our elders, learn from their struggles and triumphs, and celebrate their resilience. But we also have a responsibility to listen to younger queers, to hear their dreams, their questions and their truths, and to make space for them to grow.'

Raga's advice is to seek your people and cherish them. 'Life is richer when shared, and your identity is not just valid, it is your strength and your superpower.'

Nicola Fenton is an activist, and is also Raga's wife and podcast co-host. She tells me, 'Your life doesn't have to look like anyone else's; there is no single "lesbian template"'.

She says that in order to advocate for yourself, you need to take your health, finances and long-term happiness seriously. 'Don't wait to be "braver someday". Tell people you love them. Leave situations that drain you. Wear "that thing". Take the trip. Say no without an essay.

Regret is heavy. The world taught me many things that aren't true. Healing isn't linear. It wasn't my shame, it's not your shame.'

And again, she emphasises the notion of community: 'Younger lesbians don't need to be tougher; they need to be supported. If you ever get the chance to be that support for someone else, take it. It matters more than you think.'

Wildblood and Queenie, a DJ duo who have been together behind the decks and romantically for over three decades imparted their advice too: 'Be a peacock. Always be proud of who you are – you are fabulous. You may not feel like that right now. You may not have found your tribe. You may not fit in. But know this. One day soon, you will. The kookiness and queerness make you and will gift you the most glorious of lives. Love is coming your way. For who you are and what you will become. You will find the place you will belong and it will feel like home. A home you made – with your chosen family. A queer family that will thank their lucky disco stars they met you. We can't wait to watch you grow, to see what you become, to marvel at the life you create and the difference you will make. That's our job as queer elders. To hold our hand out and bring you with us. To watch you become the truly magnificent queer we know you to be.'

Our elders are living proof that while we can celebrate the great PR sapphics are having right now (they walked so we could run), there is still so much work to be done.

Yes, we're currently in the lesbianaissance, but let's be clear – that just means an uptick in visibility. Mainstream media has accepted Chappell Roan as a legitimate pop star, Hayley Kiyoko's 'Girls Like Girls' was so successful it has been adapted into a film, and Robby Hoffman is set to become a much less problematic Ellen. And yet, despite this representation, we still exist on the periphery. It is easy to see this as a win, which it is, but it is a win for being acknowledged, for being invited in the room, not for being treated like equals. Don't get it twisted – books and films and discussions that have existed for decades for hets are still relatively new for us.

Part of the reason I wanted to write this book was to loudly celebrate and record sapphic culture. For so long it has been written in code and squirrelled away, with sapphic leanings sniffed out through pinky rings, fleeting nods and secret symbols. In the current climate, it is important to disseminate this information, to be visible and hold fast. Lesbianism isn't a cool, quirky trend. For me and my girls, this is forever.

So go out there and live your life proudly and loudly. Foster community. Take up space. **Be dykonic.**

FAQs
FAQs
FAQs

FAQs
FAQs
FAQs

Welcome to queer queries, in which I enter my Agony Guncle era. I have long loved dishing out unsolicited advice, so it was a nice change to do so solicited. I asked you guys to send in your burning questions and sifted through them to find the most frequently asked. So, here you go!

I'm a bisexual woman with a boyfriend, and I struggle with not feeling queer enough. How do I keep in touch with my queer identity?

I don't mean to diagnose you, my darling, but you may be struggling with a little bit of internalised biphobia. Being bi means you are queer 100 per cent of the time, not just when you are visibly queer to others! Make sure you remind yourself of this. There is no 'queer enough', there is no bisexual loyalty card that you have to rack up queer acts on to maintain your queer status. You are bisexual when you have a girlfriend, when you have a boyfriend, when you have a theyfriend.

If you know all this and want something a little more tangible, you can join queer clubs, march for queer rights, go to queer nights, watch queer creators, see queer movies, hang out with your queer friends, dye your queer hair, research queer history, pierce your queer nose and, maybe, you could even read this queer book.

How can I find my community without just dating every dyke in my local area?

This is a really amazing question. I personally cannot answer this from experience, because I have, in fact, dated every dyke in my local area. You can't say I've never done anything for the community!

But the real answer is, you just need to throw yourself in. It will be scary at first but as the old adage goes: no risk, no reward. Go to your local dyke bar, and strike up a conversation. Take to TikTok, Reddit and Google to find local lesbian clubs or events in your area. You can join dating apps, but make it clear that you are just looking for queer friends. If all else fails, join a football team or start hanging around your local organic supermarket.

How do I bi-curiously experiment without accidentally taking advantage of girls?

Experimenting gets a bad wrap. We all have to start somewhere, right? I think we need to shake this idea of experimenting and think of it more as an exploration. She isn't a cadaver in a science lab begging to be poked and probed.

Explore with the best intentions. For example, you should be kissing her because you want to be kissing her, not because you want to be seen kissing her. Make sure you are conscious of her feelings while also listening to how you are feeling in the moment. Go slow, and if you aren't sure, go even slower. If you feel an urge to kiss her, and she wants to too, then do so, and if it feels great, then explore a little further and see how that feels. Then rinse and repeat. If you're feeling a little out of your depth, say so. You don't need to declare your body count before you do anything, but it could also help to say you're new to this if you need some guidance.

I've been a lesbian my whole life, so why do I now feel like I have to experiment with men?

Girl, you don't have to do anything! However, if you want to... then why not? I have been told that (theoretically) men can be (allegedly) sexually (?) attractive. It's not completely unheard of to come out as a lesbian and then double back on the scale to experiment with men. Maybe you're bi. Maybe you're somewhere totally else on the scale. That's fun! Shag who you wanna shag!

On the other hand, feeling like you need to experiment with men could also be the comphet monster rearing its ugly head. Fear not! We have a trusty tool designed to tackle this specific dilemma: an ancient dyke text known colloquially as the Lesbian Masterdoc. For those who weren't on sapphic Tumblr circa 2018, the publication of this PDF was a lesbian canon event in itself. Since its release, it has reached all corners of the sapphic world, with notable celesbians such as Reneé Rapp and Kehlani referencing it. Essentially, it's a document that aims to ask the right questions to figure out whether your sexuality may be subconsciously influenced by the heteronormative society we live in. Now, it isn't without its flaws, and it isn't backed up by actual science, but it is an interesting tool that could potentially help you understand your queerness. If you're interested, the Masterdoc PDF is still online, and easily findable with Google...

How should I approach travelling to countries with different LGBTQ+ laws?

Make sure to do your research before you book. There are a bunch of resources online that'll show you in which countries it is illegal to be gay or trans. It might be useful to check the foreign travel advice page of your own government, to see what they recommend and what precautions to take. If you are trans or non-binary, make sure to update your travel documents if possible, so that they match your physical gender expression to avoid any unnecessary attention drawn to you. When looking for accommodation, it's a good idea to book places that specifically say they are queer-friendly. The International LGBTQ+ Travel Association (IGLTA) has a whole list of recommendations.

When you're there, make sure to keep your wits about you. I know this isn't fun, but use discretion when being affectionate to your partner. In a lot of conservative countries, this is frowned upon even for the straights. Remember, safety is your priority! While these laws are obviously harmful, outdated and an infringement on human rights, you have to be respectful of them for your own wellbeing.

When should I bring up that I'm a baby gay when I'm dating someone more experienced in queer dating?

Every sapphic first date is just people talking about their coming out story, gay awakenings, celesbian crushes, etc, so I'm sure it'll come out pretty quickly. If you somehow avoid the subject, by talking about whatever celesbian has just started dating a man, or the recipe behind your favourite flaxseed, sugar-free, organic, gluten-free banana bread recipe, don't stress. Even the dykiest dyke was a baby gay once upon a time. You aren't less than because you've only just tweaked that you weren't having 'girl crushes' your whole childhood, and instead were having crushes. And if your date isn't cool with that, then they likely aren't going to be cool, period. Ditch them, and find someone more your speed.

Is it possible to overcome comphet?

The thing about comphet is that it is systemic. Society enforces comphet through media, sex education, representation and the assumption that one is straight until proven otherwise. So until we dismantle the system completely (pending), comphet is inherently unavoidable. What you can do, though, is stay queerzical (another totally made-up portmanteau by me). Questioning the intention behind our choices and the choices being made around us will bring awareness to the comphet undertones, and we can learn how to avoid avoid avoid. Consume queer media. Familiarise yourself with sapphic TV shows, content creators, films and books. Immerse yourself in sapphic culture, and slowly you will decentre the heterosexual sphere. By supporting sapphic culture, arts and community, we will also increase demand and encourage more funding, which will, in turn, dilute comphet in society.

Can I still lez out if I hate textile crafts?

Not possible, sorry!

What's the best way to handle the queer dating scene when everyone's dated everyone?

Well, honey, unless you plan on moving cities after every situationship, you're just going to have to learn to deal with it. That's kind of the gag. The lesbian web is one of the worst/most-beautiful things about being in the WLW world. My piece of advice? Don't be toxic when dating someone. Otherwise, everyone will know :)

How can I let my coworkers know I'm gay?

If you're asking this, I presume it's because you want to let them know, but it is worth saying here that you don't have to. It is totally up to you how much you do or don't reveal to your coworkers about yourself and your personal life.

When my sister first joined the company she works at, she felt uncomfortable telling everyone at work she had a girlfriend and opted to use the term 'partner' when discussing her love life. After a while, however, she felt more uncomfortable with hiding the fact that she was gay, and casually let her colleagues know. Now she is the agency's LGBTQ+ Representative in wider company EDI forums (whatever that means!) and has made her workspace just that much more inclusive to other queer people. Any apprehension you may have about coming out at work is more than understandable, since the workplace has a long history of hostility towards queer people. However, I would argue society has come a long way, even if the news headlines of late argue the opposite. This is all to say that by letting them know, something really beautiful could happen, but there is also no pressure.

How you choose to reveal it is also totally up to you. You probably don't need to have a sit-down meeting with your colleagues to divulge that you're a friend of Dorothy. Flippantly mention a date you went on where 'she' did XYZ, or find an apt moment to drop in a mention of your ex-girlfriend. Alternatively, maybe this is a good time to don those rainbow socks your mum bought you for Christmas one year.

I'm struggling with internalised homophobia. How do I work through this?

Girl... welcome. We've alllll been there. Not to be all AA about things, but acknowledgement is the first step. Congrats! Now, let's dismantle it from within. What do you think? And why do you think these things? Are they your thoughts, or society's? Make sure you are talking to yourself with kindness. Educate yourself on queer history, important figures and the fight for your rights. Watch queer shit. There's probably a whole bunch of stereotypes that you hold in your head, and positive queer media can help you unlearn them. Find community. This could be online first if it is easier for you. Shout out to all the lesbian YouTubers that I was (not so) randomly obsessed with growing up. Talk to friends and family members who you feel safe with, and who love you for you. Therapy is pretty useful for this kind of stuff too.

Eventually, you will reach a place where the pendulum swings the other way, and you actually feel superior for being a queer person. Then, like me, you will make it your whole personality and will spend every conversation waiting for the right moment to not-so-subtly drop that you're a raging lezza.

How do I cope with feeling inadequate as a femme 4 femme when competing with mascs?

Baby, baby, baby. Let me say something loud and clear: there is no pecking order when it comes to lesbians. As a femme 4 femme, you are not competing with mascs. You're not competing with anyone! Comparison is the thief of joy!

Sometimes we get a little caught up in the whole gender expression of it all. Yes, you can have a physical preference, but no one has ever fancied anyone purely based on the fact that they wear a dress or a backwards cap. One day you will find your beautiful femme 4 femme, and she will be an absolute delight, and you'll confess to her that you used to feel inadequate when competing with mascs, and she'll laugh and say that it's only ever been you.

I've fallen hard for one of my friends. Should I tell them, or let it go?

Now, this is tricky. There is no blanket rule, but you need to think about the situation with the most objective perspective you can. Is your friend queer? How important is this friendship to you? Are you prepared to potentially lose it? Do you honestly, in the bottom of your heart, think that you could be good together? Are they giving you any signals? Be real with yourself with this one. No holding onto some brushed leg under the table from weeks ago. Limerence is not your friend in this circumstance. Ultimately, I think the most important thing in this situation is how you would react in the case that your friend doesn't feel the same way. Rejection can sting and make things awkward. If you seriously think you have the ability to get rejected, brush yourself off and continue being friends with this person, then go for it. Just be prepared to swallow your ego.

My family aren't OK with me being a lesbian. How can I get past this?

Families can be tricky. Firstly, I want you to acknowledge the fact that you've been brave enough to be true to yourself in the face of adversity. That takes real grit and courage. Secondly, I want you to know that empathy goes a long way. When I was younger, as soon as someone had a different view from me, I would instantly just think they were ignorant and stupid and that we would never get along. The older I get, the more I try to understand them. This is not to say that I think they are right, but it is easier to reach common ground when you meet someone with empathy and understanding. And if we're looking at it from a selfish perspective, it does feel really good to be the bigger person when you've been wronged.

Families can often get it wrong, and they'll probably get it wrong again and again, but after a while, hopefully, they'll start getting it less wrong and more right. It's unlikely you're going to Uno-reverse the gay, so they're just going to have to get better at loving you. Family is one of the relationships that are (to an extent) worth sticking it out for, even if it is a little bumpy.

However in some cases, this really isn't an option and in order to protect yourself and your wellbeing, the best thing you can do is walk away. The beautiful thing about the queer community is that family doesn't have to be bound by blood and we can build ourselves a chosen family. Whether that's friends, mentors, partners or community members, these people see you fully, love you freely and show up for you without conditions. This is family.

How do you deal with casual homophobia?

One of my friends has this really amazing technique. When someone says something problematic, or an off-colour joke, she says, 'What do you mean?' She keeps her tone neutral but inquiring, and keeps on asking them to explain themselves until they get embarrassed. A lot of casual homophobia is rooted in harmful stereotypes. Getting the person to explain it to such a granular, unfunny degree really takes the sting out of it and reveals them to be the dickhead they are.

My partner is not as out and proud as I am. How do I handle this?

This one is sticky because people might have various reasons for not being out and proud. Safety, obviously, is pretty key. If they live in an area or with family that they feel unsafe being out and proud with, then you need to account for this. If this is a matter of internalised homophobia, that's also tricky. You can be there for them and help with resources, but you've also got to let them figure it out on their own. Lastly, remember that 'out and proud' looks different on everyone. People choose to express their queerness in a bunch of different ways. You might be the pin-wearing, flag-carrying, septum-ring-bearing type, and they might feel like they're shouting their queerness from the Timberlands they're wearing.

In relationships, there will always be compromise. However, if you harbour resentment, this can create a toxicity that will bleed into your relationship. You have to recognise where your boundaries lie and if this is something that crosses them, then the kindest thing you can do to yourself and to them is to let them go. But if they support you being as out and proud as you are, and you support them doing their thing in their own way, then you'll be fine.

Dykonic Recommendations

As I am sure you're well aware, sexuality, gender identity and queer studies in general are all very nuanced topics. Whilst this book aims to introduce you to said topics, it barely even scratches the surface. Much more in-depth analysis and specific works exist, and I urge you to explore them further.

One of my biggest hopes with this book was to elicit a thirst for more dyke consumption (not that kind of dyke consumption, you dirty bastard). With that being said, I have put together a list of sapphic recommendations, from books to read, podcasts to listen to, zines to buy and social media accounts well worth following.

Culture & Memes

@godimsuchadyke
@lesbiancinema
@everylesbianandtheirfashion
@sapphic_sandwich
@whatzaraloves
All The Things She Said by Daisy Jones
Girls Can Kiss Now by Jill Gutowitz
Pretty Gay on Patreon
Twos Two Podcast
Two Dykes and a Mic podcast

History & Education

@dressingdykes
@lesbian_herstory
@lesbianherstoryarchives
@xiaolongbby
@jessicaoutofthecloset
@tyrablizz
ContraPoints on YouTube
Binchtopia podcast
Our Dyke Histories podcast
Unsuitable: A History of Lesbian Fashion by Eleanor Medhurst
Outrage by Ellen Jones
Them magazine

Fiction Books

Milk Fed by Melissa Broder
Chosen Family by Madeleine Gray
Big Swiss by Jen Beagin
Pleasure Beach by Helen Palmer
Stone Butch Blues by Leslie Feinberg
The History of my Sexuality by Tobi Lakmaker
Rubyfruit Jungle by Rita Mae Brown

Zines & Magazines

Physical media is available, but I have listed Instagram handles for ease.

@dyke.4.dyke
@dykesanddolls
@planet.lesbian
@dirtydykemagazine
@chapstickmagazine
@xoxogossipd_yke
@anarkiss_zine
@divamagazine
@autostraddle

Community

@thedykeproject
@thelesbianmissedconnections
@dyke_directory
The Lesbian Bar Project
HER app

Index

Acknow-ledgements

I would like to start my acknowledgements, of which there are plenty – it truly takes a village (people) – by thanking all of you. Not only for your amazing contributions to the book, from your candid and hilarious sex stories to inspiring coming-out stories. But, also for your continued support for absolutely everything I do. Every comment, DM, in-person conversation. You have changed my life forever. Thank you.

To my incredible editor, Samhita Foria, firstly, I'd like to thank you for being so, so patient with me and my ADHD. For bearing with me whilst I pushed any and every deadline you set. But mostly I want to thank you for your immeasurable input and tireless work behind the scenes. Without you, this book wouldn't be here, and I wouldn't know that I was capable of pushing myself to accomplish such a thing.

And to the rest of those from the Bloomsbury team who have brought this vision to life, Eleanor Corbett as copyeditor, George Saad as designer, Joely Day as proofreader, Isobel Turton as my publicist and to everyone else on the team THANK YOU. It's such a pinch-me moment to be a Bloomsbury author!!!

To my incredible illustrator AJ. Thank you for creating such beautiful art for this project its been such a pleasure to work with you. The book wouldn't feel the same without the injection of whimsy your queer art brings.

Joss Peter, thank you so much for your tireless help and support in making this book a reality. Your queer knowledge and ability to help me make sense of my own thoughts is unmatched (wish I could say the same about your cambio skills :/). I am so grateful to have you in my life in general, and feel very lucky that we get to work together. There's no one I'd rather unpack sapphic sex scenes over a pint with. To more gossip, Pho Viet and Lana Del Rey <3

To Millie Lean and Kate Landy, I can't thank you enough for your unwavering support, attention to detail and ongoing diligence at every stage of this process. Having you both in my corner has been completely invaluable, thank you, thank you, thank you.

To Emma Lindley and the M+C Saatchi team, thank you for managing my ADHD ass so well and helping me juggle it all. I feel so at home with you.

Mum and Dad look! I'm a published author!!!! There aren't enough thanks in the world to express how grateful I am to have you as parents. Everything I am and everything I've achieved is because of the foundation you gave me. I hope this book makes you proud.

To my gorgeous dykey sisters, Sophie and Lucy. I am so lucky to have a built-in community at home. You both inspire me to celebrate my queerness unapologetically every single day. I am so proud of how far we have come in learning to love and express that part of ourselves so loudly. You will always have me in your corner.

And shout-out to my in-law sapphic sis Hattie as well. I was blessed to have two and now have three! I love you so much and thank you for constantly championing everything I do. #LesbianTable4ever

To Izzi Phillips, World's Best Ex Girlfriend, thanks for not only dragging me out of the closet (who knows where I'd be without you) but thank you for being my on-call sapphic expert whenever I needed a reference cross-checked. You are one of my closest friends and I am so grateful to still have you in my life.

To my best mates Abster and Eliza , thank you for your constant support, for reminding me to keep going when things felt overwhelming and for always being on hand with giggles at the ready. I'd be lost if I didn't have you both by my side.

Rupert McMinn, the world's greatest dyke ally. I have never had someone so in my corner. I'm in awe of you, and it's such a privilege to not only work with you but also call you a best friend.

And finally, to my much better half, Catty. You've taught me so much about queer love, queer joy, and all that has gone into shaping this book. You make me want to be the best version of myself and your support and belief in everything I do keep me going, even on the days I doubt myself. Forever my girl. Caru chdi bug.

BLOOMSBURY PUBLISHING
Bloomsbury Publishing Plc
50 Bedford Square, London, WC1B 3DP, UK
29 Earlsfort Terrace, Dublin 2, Ireland

BLOOMSBURY, BLOOMSBURY PUBLISHING and the Diana logo are trademarks of Bloomsbury Publishing Plc

First published in Great Britain 2026

A catalogue record for this book is available from the British Library

Library of Congress Cataloguing-in-Publication data has been applied for [Add where a UK originated single-ISBN edition for which we own US rights]

ISBN: HB: 978-1-0372-0201-8; eBook: 978-1-0372-0204-9

10 9 8 7 6 5 4 3 2 1

Commissioning Editor: Samhita Foria
Copyeditor: Eleanor Corbett
Proofreader: Joely Day
Designer: George Saad
Illustrator: AJ Duncan
Production: Ben Chisnall

Printed and bound in the UK by Clays Ltd, Elcograf S.p.A

Bloomsbury Publishing Plc makes every effort to ensure that the papers used in the manufacture of our books are natural, recyclable products made from wood grown in well-managed forests. Our manufacturing processes conform to the environmental regulations of the country of origin.

To find out more about our authors and books visit www.bloomsbury.com and sign up for our newsletters. For product safety related questions contact productsafety@bloomsbury.com

Oooh
LGBT